PUBLISHED BY TRANSCENDENT ZERO PRESS

www.transcendentzeropress.org

ISBN: 978-1-946460-21-9

Printed in the United States of America

Library of Congress Control Number: 2019955499

Cover photo: Live photo from Woodshock 1986 by Jerry "Dog" Schadle, first published in the Daily Texan, Austin, August 1987.

Book illustrations by Nazrul Islam Ripon/Flickr via CC

Thanks to Erica Renteria for archival scanning.

FIRST EDITION

TRANSCENDENT ZERO PRESS

DISCOGRAPHY 1980s

Peace Corpse (1986)
Yuppie Poster Child-Peace Corps (1987)
A Distant Land to Roam-KJ solo-(1987)
Living in a Bourgeois Town-Peace Corps (1988)
Land of No Purpose-KJ solo (1989)
Heart Attacks and Lies-KJ solo (recorded 1989, released 1991)
Pastures of Plenty-Ken Jones and Peace Corps LP (1989)
"In a Cocked Rifle's Crack" Glitch Sampler #4 1988

Some of the music for these song lyrics is available on SoundCloud under either the Austin's Peace Corps or PoetKen Jones 80s Song Lyrics accounts.

BAND MEMBERS, MUSICIANS, AND SONGWRITING COLLABORATORS:

Mitch Ginsburg (guitar and bass) P.C. 1985-1989)
Mike Sekula (lead guitar) P.C. 1985-1986
Gene Huang (bass and guitar)-P.C. 1985-1989
Tennyson LeMaster (R.I.P.) (drums)1985-1986
Rob Cooley (drums)-P.C 1986-1989
Greg "Psychohippie" Jones (R.I.P.) 1988
Steve Vague (saxophone) 1986-1988
Jonathan Flothow (saxophone) 1986-1988
Walter Daniels (harmonica) 1987-1989 solo tapes
Kyle Rosenblad (guitar) 1987-1989 solo tapes
Jimmy Juup (guitar) 1987-1989 solo tapes
Michael Fogle (bass) 1989 solo tape
Mike Alvarez (guitar) 1989 solo tape
Byron "Siren" Scott (R.I.P.) solo and P.C. 1988-1989

(Apologies for any errors or omissions. And eternal thanks to the sound engineers, booking agents, club owners, studio owners, photographers, journalists, flyer artists, fellow poets and musicians, and many others whose work appears here, too numerous to mention in this brief space or lost in the fog of memory, as well as all those who helped create the times documented here)

Austin in the 1980s was a uniquely free environment to come of age as both a person and a creative artist. Rents were cheap, with plenty of people and places to party and perform and, most importantly, with an open minded live and let live vibe that encouraged experimentation and interaction.

I arrived in 1981 from Corpus Christi with a National Merit Scholarship paying my way at UT as an English Major and a drive to make a career as a poet. As quixotic as that sounds in hindsight, Austin was the ideal incubator for such an infantile ambition. As I progressed into publishing and performing poetry, I also was an avid music fan who attended hundreds of the great shows that flowed through Austin in that era. I was also beginning to transform some of my poems into song lyrics, jamming in lofts and living rooms with college friends. Frankly, we weren't very good, but even then, we had a blast and seeing as I had written piano songs ever since my junior high school days, I found music as an outlet fulfilling in its own way.

We had so much time to play that Malcolm Gladwell's 10,000 hours of practice rule began to manifest itself. I remember at one point in 1984 realizing I was writing some songs (with others playing guitar and me singing) I could actually stand to listen to. I started regularly attending shows at a local music dive called The Beach Cabaret, where some of my friends were bartenders, and meeting many others who were so influential in the music that this book documents. One of those people, Jerry "Dog" Schadle, worked at Kinko's on the Drag so he used the copiers to create a zine FLYING HORSE, in which I began publishing poetry and later song lyrics. He also hosted live multimedia gigs at the Beach called FLYING HORSE SYMPOSIUMS, and asked me to start reading poetry opening for some of the leading underground bands of the time.

Everyone in Austin then seemed to be making music, so we also decided to form a band and headed to a storage unit to practice. Hence Peace Corpse/Peace Corps/Peace Corp. was born. As this book documents, from 1985-1989 we recorded a fairly substantial catalogue of original songs and I also began working with those and other musicians on a series of solo projects -which we released on cassette

tapes and sold at local record stores. We also were fortunate enough to play live at almost every venue in Austin that allowed original music, and made our own small mark on the local alternative music scene-as dozens of other bands of that era did. As you'll see by reading these pages, I was able to save a substantial amount of memorabilia from that time-throwing it in a Rubbermaid container that I stored in my childhood room (Thanks Mom [insert blow kiss emoji]). Now that I've entered late middle age, and have seen some of the most well known musicians of that era pass away, I decided it was time for this material to see the light of day. I view this book as a personal history, obviously, but also as a slice of life archive of a particular era in Austin history. Call it one man and one band's view of a time and place that holds so many memories for so many-and take it as my humble offering to those who were there to trigger your own reflections.

My thanks here go first and foremost to all whose work is included here (see the Endnotes and Discography page for names, places, and some of the details my aging mind can remember) and, of course, all my bandmates and songwriting collaborators. I also want to thank Dustin Pickering and His Transcendent Zero Press whose genuine interest and encouragement in what some might view as a vanity project gave me the energy to plow forward. Thanks also to Susie Tommaney, whose graphic design and layout skills have been pivotal in so many of my publishing projects.

Mitch Ginsburg, my stalwart friend and bandmate, was there at the beginning 35 years ago with his original chord progressions that became many of these songs, and assisted with scanning the original documents. And to both him and Spyder Angelo-my current music producer-who has digitized and remastered much of the music here from old cassette tapes at his Sound Street Studios in Houston-my great gratitude for your unwavering support.

Finally, I salute all of those contemporaries from 1980s Austin-many of whom went on to progress much farther in the music industry than we ever did-for their contribution to making Austin the music Mecca it became.
PoetKen Jones 11-25-19

The Way Life Goes

Lyrics

Lyrics with graphics

Flyers

Press

SIDE ONE

A DISTANT LAND TO ROAM (JONES)

Last night I dreamed we left here for good
Got out of town at sundown, as far away as we could
Fields of goldenrod unrolled beauty unsurpassed
A chance to touch the taste of freedom at last
  (CHORUS) Every mother's son dreams of leaving home
                For a distant land
                A distant land to roam
                Somewhere out there there must be a place for us

Last night I held you and told you of my dream
Your bright eyes grew wider, I swore I saw them gleam
As I poured forth the story, I saw your smile turn scary
You buried your hair in my chest and whispered, "Please take me"
        (CHORUS)
So tonight give me your hand, we'll face this distant place
Try to understand the emptiness behind its pretty face
We will live dissipated in the shadow of our father's failure
Believe in our love as the only certain cure
        (CHORUS)

THE ALIEN (GINSBURG/JONES)

At the roadblock, there were gringos
Flashing badges, guns gleaming
They let go all the Anglos
I could hear my brothers screaming
Out the bus they led us one by one
Lined us up like cattle in the sun
Pushed us down to the ground hard
And asked to see our green card
  (CHORUS) To them, I'm just an alien
          A piece of paper makes me human

There was no hope in my homeland
So on foot I crossed the desert
Why can't these soldiers understand
How much that journey hurt
If they could only be me
At the other end of the gun
Maybe then they'd finally see

The choices that forced me to run
    (CHORUS)
My wife, she's eight months pregnant
Waiting for the day in the barrio
Now these men want us sent
Back to a pain they'll nevber know
And I hope they can sleep at night
Knowing they've taken my child's right
To grow up free of poverty
I'll remember when he goes to bed hungry
    (CHORUS)

SHARE THE NIGHTMARE (ROSENBLAD/JONES)

When the solace of the morning
Meets the treason of the evening
Our closeness will keep us from harm
And we'll share the nightmare
As if we were spared
By the warmth of each other's arms
  (CHORUS)   Run to me and you will see
                    Run to me and you will see
                    That my love for you's a river
                    Let it flow eternally

Crack the curtain of the broken window
See a shallow world of sorrow
A void to keep us apart
A chant of fire through my heart
Burning hungry and unsung
    (CHORUS)

SONG TO JIMMIE (JUPP/JONES)

From the town of Meridian, in the year of '29
He sang of where the water tastes like cherry wine
He rode those freights to the end of the line
Where a Victor man was waitin' with a contract to sign
  (CHORUS)   So hey, hey, Jimmie Rodgers, I wrote you a song
                    Though you've been down in the ground so long

He yodeled his heart through tubucular lungs
Wandered the counties with his guitar slung
Over his shoulders and his conductor's cap hung

Down in his eyes like the songs he sung
        (CHORUS)
His blue yodels filled backwoods radios
Farm boys mesmerized by the firelights glow
Gripped by the awe of things they didn't know
A piece of relief from the hard road they'd hoe
        (CHORUS)
To Texas he came when his voice flowed golden
With his blue Caddilac and Blue Yodeler's Mansion
And it was true when he said he could get more women
Than a train could haul---and all from his singin'
        (CHORUS)

        WIDE BEAUTIFUL EYES (JONES)

In your wide beautiful eyes
I see green fields and blue skies
I see rivers raging in waves
I see a fire so bright it saves
In your wide beautiful eyes
I see a world where life is right
I see afear so fierce it cries
For me to quiet its dark light

In your soft sumptuous arms
I feel a haven from all harm
I feel a heaven real and warm
And a chapel of sweet charms
In your wide beautiful eyes
In your wide beautiful eyes

        TRACES OF NATURE (GINSBURG/JONES)

Every road we ride down
Was laid by hard hands
There are no free footfalls in this land
Every path we wander down
Been totally explored before
There are no virgin pathways anymore
Every river we conquer
Powers myriad mechanical hands
There are only traces of nature in this land
Every home we hide in
Warm wombs without sin
Leads us to believe in free rides

In this hard land, In this hard land
In this hard land, In this hard , hard, land

SIDE TWO

OCCUPIED AMERICA (GINSBURG/JONES)

A jarring wake-up call---gunfire sings
I scream---then listen as alarm bells ring
Too much in this world I don't understand
The bitter, hateful way man treats man
So drop your books and into the street
Let';s dance away our sure defeat
Rockin' pneumonia, rollin' hysteria
Occupied America, Occupied America

In this land of Man's it's hard to find
A way to escape peace of mind
We slave away from the first crack of dawn
So they gaze on peaceful, manicured lawns
From Harlem to Lincoln, Nebraska
Occupied America, Occupied America

Here in our human paradise
Everything has a price

LIVE TO DIE (JUPP/JONES)

A dirty town where sound surrounds
Asphalt spaces shrouding ground
Our clean white faces still haven't found
The alleys truth's been hunted down
    (CHORUS)   The engines of sin are grinning
                You and I, You and I, You and I, Live to die
                Feel the heat of the waste of winning
                You and I, You and I, You and I, Live to die

From a cloudy valley we hear
The haunted, hungry voices of fear
Moans our clean minds cannot bear
These quiet nights where we share our fear
        (CHORUS)
I see your eyes in dreams I have
Fields of paradise in schemes I gave

These dog days---a vain hope to save
Your eyes' light from an early grave
    (CHORUS)

   I DON'T BELONG (GINSBURG/JONES)

Window shopping at the women's clothing store
She stares at shoes she needs; her feet are sore
Locked out by her empty pocketbook
All she can do is look
She cries as she spies
The rows of new clothes
On her back, a tattered blanket
Over polyester trousers
She understands wants
She had dreams once
And she screams,
"I don't belong, I don't belong
What's going on, it's so wrong
For me to see everybody happy
When I don't belong, I don't belong"

Hanging out at the local watering hole
She sips her fifth drink; she's lost control
Hungry but her money goes to ease her hurt
All she wants is comfort
She cries as she lies
Alone again at home
On her back a tattered blanket
The sheets wear a desolate scent
She understands wants
She had dreams once
And she screams
"I don't belong, I don't belong
What's going on, it's so wrong
For me to see everybody happy
When I don't belong, I don't belong"

   LAST CALL AT THE LOST CAUSE (DANIELS/JONES)

A man dreams of running away
A woman dreams of her wedding day

   SOMEDAY NEVER COMES
    (JOHN FOGERTY)

PEACE (JONES)

Hide
Hide from the battle
Hide from the pain
Breathe
Breathe deep and smile
The world's not insane
It's the only way it can be
Forget immortality
You can't change the world
Settle for survival
Comfortable and free
Just you and me
Arms around each other
Let your warmth smother me
Peace
Peace to all people
You'll all end like me

ALL LYRICS BY KEN JONES
 MUSICIANS:
Middle Walter Daniels: Harmonica on 1,2,4,
                        Flute on 6, 10
Mitch Ginsburg: Acoustic guitar on 2,6,7,9
Jimi Jupp: Bass on 3,4,8; Acoustic guitar on 11
            Backing vocals on 2,4,7,8,11
Ken Jones: Piano on 1,5,12; Backing vocals on 1,2,5,6,7,10.11
Kyle Rosenblad: Acoustic guitar on 3,4,8

    Engineered by Kyle Rosenblad on Willie Khomeini's Fostex 4-track
    All selections copyright 1987 by Ken Jones

    1. A DISTANT LAND TO ROAM 2.THE ALIEN 3. SHARE THE NIGHTMARE
    4. SONG TO JIMMIE 5.WIDE BEAUTIFUL EYES 6. TRACES OF NATURE
    7. OCCUPIED AMERICA 8. LIVE TO DIE 9. I DON'T BELONG 10. LAST
    CALL AT THE LOST CALL 11. SOMEDAY NEVER COMES 12. PEACE
AAA
  A A DISTANT LAND TO ROAM
        KEN JONES

]

DRESS CODE

You can wear your hair
Any way you want
Neatly layered in place
Teased or a bouffant
We care more about your clothes
We enforce a strict dress code

A button down shirt for men
Neatly tucked in
Skirts showing a little skin
Are fine for women
And high-heeled shoes to torture your toes
We enforce a strict dress code

A missing button
Or collar slightly frayed
And we'll surely shun you
Like you haven't been paid
No cut-off shorts or hems unsewed
We enforce a strict dress code

Bop in hot pink boxers
With leg warmers hugging you
Modern bobby soxers
With nothing bugging you
Cruising blindly down the easy road
You enforce a strict dress code

PASTURES OF PLENTY

Disturbed in your suburb
Down the asphalt we rolled
And the houses were mountains
The streets valleys so cold
We stood open mouthed
Dreaming it was ours
But knew that it was all due
To whitewashed golden towers
Pastuures of Plenty, Pastures of Plenty

And the backs of the millions
Creaked and echoed with pain
To make these playland streets
Seem pristine and sane
On the edge of your city
We saw concrete created
The workers moved in unison
Dull hollow eyes that hated
Pastures of Plenty, Pastures of Plenty

A long asphalt road our poor feet have trod
Walking concrete and clay, hard stone and sod
And comfort's products strewn as far as we could see
These brick, electric caves were pastures of plenty
Pastures of plenty, pastures of plenty

A Taste of the Wild

She don't care about her hair
She don't worry about what she wears
(Chorus) She's just a part of nature, just another creature
Just a part of nature, just another creature
But in each other's arms we somehow sense a cure
I just want to baby her

All she needs are her eyes and a smile
To feed this hungry boy a taste of the wild
        (Chorus)
She don't follow phony fashion
Her heart leads her with true passion
        (Chorus)

The Blind Child

Last night I couldn't settle down to sleep
I lay awake, shivering in the inside cold
And I remembered when I was two-years-old
Swimming suspended in the six-foot deep
   (Chorus) We're just killing time
               Bend the mind of the blind child

The bottom dropped out from my tiny feet
Thrashing at the stifling covers
I screamed for the arms of my Father
Spitting and ripping my sheets
            (Chorus)

Mother ran in from the next room
Sobbing, "Oh, God, not again"
I knew I'd seen things then
~~████████████~~ understand
So as am I'd   (Chorus)

BIRTH DEFECT

I came out hungry and knowing nothing
A passionate moment's accident
I grew up quiet but knowing something
Ugly lingered under the oxygen tent
Half in love with easeful Death
But grasping for every gasping breath
I saw so much to reject
I guess it's just a birth defect

I came out healthy and looked unscarred
An unqualified genetic success
I grew up quiet but stared hard
At the world's incurable distress
Discontent etched in my eyes
Consumed by the vacuum of lies
I saw so much to reject
I guess it's just a birth defect

I came out lonely and looked around
For some settled sense of safety
I grew up quiet until I found
You could be blood and breath to me
Loneliness met its timely death
In the warmth I felt in your every breath
We share so much to reject
I guess it's just a birth defect

IN A COCKED RIFLE'S CRACK

We kissed and caressed as the storm bore down
Sheltered like the blood of slaughter
Splattered on a wedding gown
Our skin the veil the fear of night tore down
(Chorus) I'm holding on to the storm's wet kiss
I'm holding on tight like this

Solitary moments melted
And we lay flat like wax
In new forms molded
On a candle's smooth back
The flame a shaman's mantra chanted
In a fight against eternal fright
Outside atmospheric torment
An ominous portent
    (Chorus)
Repeat first verse

WATCH HER SQUAT

I want to watch her squat
It gets me really hot
And when I see her pee
It sends shivers right through me
Her scars are Desire's angels
I live for a shot of her snot
To playfully fluff her dandruff
Then watch her squat
Her urine sweet sweet syrup to me
I accept the waste of her body
As necessary for her beauty

SIDE TWO

CALL ME JOHN HENRY

John Henry's the name
Standin' tall is my game
I'm just a working man
Who loves to work on the women
(Chorus) 'John Henry, John Henry'
All the town girls sing
'John Henry, John Henry'
We love that thing you bring"

Sometimes I'm a soft touch
Then I ain't too much
But when I'm feelin' hard, baby,
I grow the whole nine yards
    (Chorus)
Now when they hear his name
All the women listen
They now they're engine just don't run the same
When they're missing his piston
    (Chorus)

GOD BLESSED AMERICA   by Woody Guthrie

This land is your land, this land is my land
From California to the New York Island
From the redwood forest to the Gulf Stream waters
God Blessed Amereica for me and you
As I went walking that ribbon of highway
I saw above me the endless skyway
I saw below me that golden valley
God Blessed America for me and you

THE PINNACLE TO THE PANHANDLE

In the Midland desert
A starched white shirt
Is no guarantee of prosperity
Is no guarantee of prosperity
In the Eastern pines
Mr. Three-piece suit and tie
Pines for the old economy
He pines for the old economy

Beneath Houston's oaks
Modern robber barons choke
As the oil spill kills new money
The oil spill kills new money
The debutantes and dilettante
Suffer from their lack of want
Their diamonds break the teeth of the hungry
Their diamonds break the teeth of the hungry

In trailer homes on barren fields
Children survive on only one meal
Where the hungry and the homeless
And the beaten, weak, and hopeless
Unite to quit trying and die
They unite to quit trying and die
From the Pinnacle to the Panhandle
From the Pinnacle to the Panhandle

Memphis, Tennessee

I was driving around outside of Memphis
When I learned life was something quite precious
Battered children's pictures flashed in my mind
I felt it was some kind of divine sign
So I said, "This land is my savior
This land is my friend
We all need a savior
We all need a friend."

I was driving around outside of Mobile, Alabama
I dreamed the road was littered with mothers and their children
I said, "This land is just what you need
This land will keep your kids fed
This land is your savior
This land is your friend
We all need a savior
We all need a friend."

I was driving around outside of Little Rock,,Arkansas
And you wouldn't believe what I saw
I saw starving black children eating off the street
Oh, my God, can this still be
And this land is their savior
This land is their friend
This land is quite precious
I think as I drive outside of memphis, Tennessee

Wishes for the Sixties

Paisleys and pastels adorn her body
Plastic beads and big earrings look "groovy"
But her views are skewered by the scythe
Of false perceptions gleaned from her insulated life
She wishes for the Sixties
She remembers from T.V.
A land of go-go booted cool chicks
Living just for fun
Her wishes for the Sixties
Are ignorant of history
The same ideals that opened society
Doomed their goals to failure
Wishes for the Sixties
Wishes for the Sixties

His beard and backpack lack dignity
But he's made his niche at the University
His demonstration days are drunken memories
Swallowed in his modern well-fed hypocrisy
His wishes for the Sixties
Disappeared like cotton candy
In the land of selfish Man
Battling for subsistence
His wishes for the Sixties
Were ignorant of history
The same ideals that opened society
Doomed their goals to failure
Wishes for the Sixties
Wishes for the Sixties

The Only Question

Put your foot down
The planet turns
Stare in the mirror
Your soul burns
And surely will
Go straight to hell
When those sleeping pills
Dive in for the kill
How much did you have to swallow
Before you could take no more?

I didn't ask to be born in this world
Was it worth my mother's painful contortions
Or the infinite years of society's tortures
I wish I'd been born an abortion
Taken away with the morning trash
Worth three hundred dollars cash
At least then I'd be worth something
And that's how I answer the only question
How much did you have to swallow
Before you could take no more?

The Devil's Workshop

Frowns formed in pumpkin faces
Jack o'latern potato heads
Quiet shrouded suburban places
Humanity famine kills them dead
Window with face flourescent
Only knowledgable on the block
Warted warlock pays the rent
Gives plastic near him shock
With Irish incantations loud
In voodoo, black, walrus mask
Full length KKK sheet shroud
He prepares to enter holy task
Tears open door in total costume
Tiny toddlers thrust torn sacks
Warlock screeches, hacks, shows broom
Vocal, psychological, philosophical attack.
Dilated minature eyeballs stare
Fighting to flee for the street
Warlock before returning to nightmare
Throws raisins like ~~poose~~ roses at their feet.

Fraternal Acceptance vs. Cartesian Doubt

Who is this dude, Rene Descartes?
What's so original about what he thought?
I've thought things that are just as deep.
How about this one- to dream is to sleep.
I know I exist because I think.
I know when I blow in the kitchen sink.
I exist when I put on my pink Izod.
My money proves that there is a God.
What is the point in reading this shit?
Everyone knows everything exists.
Things I can see, hear, feel, and touch.
Exist as certainly as th Brady Bunch.
Marsha exists-- she gives head to Peter.
Cindy exists- - she rides parking meters.
I accept everything, there's no cause to doubt,
T.V. tells me what it's all about.
Who gives a fuck about Rene Descartes?
Me and my frat brothers is just as smarts.

Thinking

All aboard! to a new America

Another mid-week afternoon
Pre-Happy Hour diversion
Lives bursting at the seams
Flicker only on the screen
Does his disease have a cure?
Did he really sleep with her?
Another world to ponder over
One life to live not my own
The world turns-- and I watch
Tell me what happens so I can catch up
Conserving trees to save America
I won't read-- vile dead paper
Or sit staring-- a stupid sloth
Doning naught-- but thinking
Thinking

Death Row

Pacing and pivoting back and forth,
In a six by nine foot cell.
Sometimes seems like the bottom circle,
I feel like a mutant from hell.
On a cloud shrouded evening in June,
Chicken my life's favorite game.
Whiskey shots, a couple of Mandrax,
I didn't remember my name.
They tell me I waved a twelve guage,
Stopped a van on Interstate Ten.
Blew the driver away through the windshield,
Raped his wife, then killed again.
The state says it's convenient to lie,
When I say I don't remember.
They say I received a monstrous pleasure,
Watching the couple dismembered.
No one feels any sorrow for me,
It's all talk of victim's rights.
But what will happen to my family,
When they switch shuts out my lights?

THE BRIDGE (Alvarez-Jones)

We drove across
This steel strait-jacket
As I gripped the upholstery
And the city lights beneath
Twinkled like Christmas tinsel
In a firmament sprinkled with spots
Of incomprehensible wonder
A city's fiery hunger
  (CHORUS) The Bridge, The Bridge
          Beneath the Seeds of Man
          Hard river runs
          Between father and son

Now things are so unstable
Nothing to hold onto
Except the strength of two together
When the weary day is through
And I know the lights I saw that night
Were bloody hearts burning to ignite
In volcanic triumph
But slowly melting down instead
     (CHORUS)

THE PEACE CORPS READER (Ginsburg-Jones)

The Quietmouth American
Sees an African season
Not comprhending this squalor
Is more in his character
Than saint-like motives
Or the way he used to live
  (CHORUS) Now he believes in grief
          Opening his eyes

                Stretching his mind
                In the Peace Corps
                A revolutionary force
                Peters into reality

The Quietmouth American
Thrown on the edge of Asia
Faces old fences freely
He's a long, long way
From Old Camp Shawnee
        (CHORUS)

RAVE ON (Ginsburg-Jones)

Every morning I arise
Rub my weary eyes
Take a quick shower
Then drive to this glass tower
Then I talk to folks
Try to make some deals
I'm the steady spoke
In the center of the wheel
  (CHORUS) Rave on, it's a crazy feeling
              Rave on, it's a crazy feeling

Every afternoon I head
To a downtown happy hour
Down a few scotch ans sodas
Stare up at these towers
Not thinking of the hard hands
That laid the foundation
Or the broken backs and minds
Littered through the nation
    (CHORUS)
Every night I lay down
In a room without a sound
But sleep won't come, I toss and turn
So restless my heart burns

This comfort is my birthright
And it hurts to still the rebel fight
But what I want is to belong
In the dark heart of this town
      (CHORUS)

LOVE ME (Jones)

And you won't grab my hand
And I can't even stand
And you won't even see
How you want me to be
How I can't understand
Why you won't love me

And you won't hear me out
As I pour my heart out
And you can't see I'm scared
Of a world without hope
Except for your beauty
But you just won't love me

And I can't even cry for you
And I can't even cry

Now I can't still my tears
Though they've fallen for years
Throughout history
You won't share them with me
You won't care for me
You just won't love me

DREAMS OF HEAVEN (Scott-Ginsburg-Jones)

Dreams are the reason
For the heaven sleep seems
The hell of failure
Colors their seams

Some dream of a smothering love
Some dream of a comforting above

Some dream that the world is theirs
In the spaces in their vacant stares

Some dream of warm arms
Protecting them from harm
A heaven of clothes and food
Can make this bad world good

Dreams are the reason
For the heaven sleep seems

DESPERATE TO FEEL (Ginsburg-Jones)

We have come to this place where the river powers the wheels
Desperate to feel, Desperate to feel
Numb as the cracked land, Frost hardens our hands
Desperate to feel, Desperate to feel
On the horizon tomorrow's ruins rise
Desperate to feel, Desperate to feel
  (CHORUS) We kneel then touch like mothers
            Kissing their son's corpses
            Together as brother and sister
            In this land of no purpose

We have come to this place where concrete meets steel
Desperate to feel, Desperate to feel
Above us rise business hives, vessels for all our lives
Desperate to feel, Desperate to feel
A battle to kill the fire of my eyes
Desperate to feel, Desperate to feel
    (CHORUS)

SHE BREATHES LIFE TO ME (Scott-Ginsburg-Jones)

Her brown bangs hang in noose-like strands
Gently dropping to her brow
The airy poise in how she stands
Is what I think of now
As I hide behind this building
Watching her glide by
I want her more than anything
For this love, I've gladly died

        (CHORUS) She means more than life itself to me
                She breathes life to me eternally
Her eyes revolve in glancing circles
Lively, searching for perfection
The vision collapses with a gentle pull
She cannot find my affection
As she slips beneath a canvas awning
Reflection rising in the glass door
Her ephemeral form in me spawning
Something stronger than before
        (CHORUS)

SMORGASBORD (From the Elvis Presley LP Spinout)

LAND OF NO PRUPOSE

Engineered by Mike Alvarez
Musicians:
Mike Alvarez: Acoustic and slide guitar on 1, Drums on 3
Mitch Ginsburg: Acoustic guitar on 2,3 ; bass on 5,6,7
Ken Jones: Vocals on all tracks; piano on 4
Byron Scott: Acoustic guitar on 5,6,7,8

1.The Bridge2.The Peace Corps Reader3.Rave On4.Love Me
5.Dreams of Heaven6.Desperate to Feel7.She Breathes Life
To Me8.Smorgasbord

ALL LYRICS BY KEN JONES
ENGINEERED BY MIKE ALVAREZ

Crazy and Shy

Baby, glance my way as you slither down the street
Don't be cruel to a love-struck fool
The blue suede shoes strapped to my feet
Escape you notice because you're too cool.
My blood bubbles when you slide by
I look like I'm crazy, but I'm really just too shy.

Can't you see I'm trying to get to you
Don't hide your face where I'm staring at your blouse
For all my invitations, there's nothing I can do
You're too mature to just want to play house
Can't you see what I want in my burning eyes
I look like I'm crazy, but I'm really just too shy.

Baby what does it take to make you see
That I'd rather be dead than have another girl
My crazy crush on you is maybe crushing me
But you're the greatest beauty in my filthy world
I swear I'm trying as hard as I can try
I look like I'm crazy, but I'm really just too shy.

Nine to Five Attack

Beaten at fifteen
I fled Moline
Fifty dollars in my pocket
A one-way Amtrak ticket
Through the middle of our land I rode
A drink in one hand but an empty load
~~On my back~~
~~Free of the nine to five attack~~
~~Yeah, you see the things I lack~~
~~But I'm glad and I ain't goin' back~~
~~To the mindless grind of the nine to five attack~~

← Nine to five, nine to five

With a baby a twenty
I had no money
Job at a convenience store
On the dirty Texas shore
Through the middle of our house I rage
My wife screams, "Act your age"
~~Then I crack~~
~~Stuck in the nine to five attack~~
~~Yeah, you see the things I lack~~
~~And I'm goin' mad but I can't go back~~
~~From the mindless grind of the nine to five attack~~

John Jones

ON THE EDGE

Now the factory hand makes wheels
So the farmer plows these fields
Then the grain's taken to market
And in warehouses sits
"Till a bakery company comes
And buys it to transform
The grain like magic into bread
To keep everyone along the line well-fed
But here on the edge
Bumming crumbs makes a man unstrung

Now the landman searches maps
Then gives the rancher cash
And the roustabouts dig a well
Where the men in glass towers tell
Till an oil company comes
And buys it to transform
The oil like magic into gas
To fuel the march of progress
But here on the edge
Panhandling fuel turns good men cruel

Dance Chant

March into line, my little friend
This kind of mind will never end
Follow the hollow crowd, the hollow crowd
Genuflect before the latest trend

The beat is freedom like a noose
Tight reality has no use
Deep inside the dance chant you choose
Xcited, Xcstatic, you feel loose
          You belong, you sing the song
          You belong, you sing the song

The strobe light like a campfire
Dangles in this jungle lair
The ancient electricity of desire
Sparks between each dancing pair
          You belong, you sing the song

The Fidelity Employee

Every day I smile at a thousand clean white faces
When they come to this place to check their balances
In my Oxford shirt and tie, I'm decked out to the nines
When folks ask me how I'm doin', I just answer "Fine"
(CHORUS) I'm an employee of Fidelity
        This glass tower's my security

Some days I dream of bein' its president
Then these glass towers seem heaven sent
So when I climb in my comfort chariot
The black landscape don't seem so desolate
        (Chorus)

Every night a few brews calms me down
Spend my time just flipping those channels around
From my couch one box controls the world
All I need now is a pretty little girl
        Then I'll have my security
        As an employee of Fidelity

Ken Jones

AB AC A B A'me C

BOURGEOIS BLUES

Well, he's a bourgeois man
Living in a bourgeois town
Neat streets greet his gaze
Nothing here gets him down
Miles of manicured ground
Stretch to the horizon
Not a spot left open
'Cause nothing here gets him down
(CHORUS) Nothing here gets him down (3)
            Nothing here gets him down (3)

Well, your toil on the soil
And your sweat in the steel mill
Your hot breath mechanically
Moving to lay a brick
Laid him like a saved baby
In this protected niche
A clean American room
In a bourgeois town

PARTYING FRANK

With my B.M.W. in park
I light out for the party in the dark
With my Ray-bans and button down shirt
I look like I'd never play in dirt
My daddy's rich, too
He could buy and sell you
Like you were candy hearts
Inside the shopping cart
(CHORUS) Cause I'm a Partying Frank

Parties like this with terrific friends
And I always party to the party's end
It's a blast to be in fraternities
With all these extracurricular activities
Drank two bottles
Straight Mexican tequila
Watch out below
Watch me blow
    (CHORUS)
Stains on my monogram tie clasp
Vomit stings my skin like an asp
And in my head a crazy feeling
Just what is this drunken night revealing
My throat torn
My stomach shorn
The noise of death's deafening
From alcoholic poisoning
    (CHORUS)
If I could live another day
I'd find me a sorority girl to lay
They're all the same, bleach-blonde Susies
Bland and brainless, at least they're easy
Stupidity, in my hazing
Mistakes made, my heart is blazing
Slight slip to unconsciousness
My frat house is the best

Her moans echoed like it was the Grand Canyon
Menage a Trois

Cover "concept" and photos by David L. Wilson

Consumption Blues

Consumption got hold on me
Consumption got a hold on me
Thought it was just a cough, but it was T.B.
Got me some whiskey, I'm dying to consume
Got me some whiskey, I'm dying to consume
Got too many bad thoughts to stay in this room
Wanna crawl on my belly,'cross the cold tile floor
Wanna crawl on my belly, 'cross the cold tile floor
~~Wanna beat my woman, then lay me a whore~~   *Bad thoughts...*
~~Got something mighty trembling here in my hand~~
~~Got something mighty trembling here in my hand~~
~~I called it John Henry, she calls it my middle wand~~
Bad thoughts spread 'cross my mind like jelly
Bad thoughts spread 'cross my mind like jelly
Guess that Old Man Satan ~~lives and breathes in me~~
Preacher ~~says~~ redemption is the only way
Preacher says redemption is the only way
But I say consumption lets you get through your days (Those awful
                                                    bad days)
When I die of this fever that makes me run wild
When I die of this fever that makes me run wild
Gonna have a little girl and bottle right by my side
That consumption killing me by degrees
That consumption killing me by degrees   *(chorus)*
This dissipation finally gonna set me free

Ken Jones

Your Bright Smile

Like the rivers, the mountains, the seas
I see you reflected in all these
And I'm here on my bended knees
Begging you baby, "Pretty please"
    To fill your eyes with life for a while
    To light this place with your bright smile

This morning old feelings born anew
I awoke holding you
The heart in my chest beat strong and true
So intense I thought it'd bust on through
    To fill your eyes with life for a while
    To light this place with your bright smile

In the very air, my every breath
Your beauty stills my restlessness
Before this gray winter's day turns black
I'll be gone but I swear I'm comin' back
    To fill your eyes with life for a while
    To light this place with your bright smile

Ken Jones

Native Son

I am your native son
I belong to this town
Like the ground, like the round
Clock atop the Baptist sanctuary
You cannot deny me
You will never deny me
And I am your understanding son
I long to settle down
After I conquer these fears
Of never breaking free
You cannot deny me
You will never deny me
Helping to save
The face of the community
A neighborhood penetentiary
A neighborhood insanity
You cannot deny me
You will never deny me
I am your native son
I belong to this town
Like the ground, like the round
Clock atop the Baptist sanctuary
You cannot deny me
You will never deny me

The Punk and Hippy Ditty

The rainbow punk girl and hippie freak
Meet at a door
The freak, a geek of epic proportions
Asks why she's sore
And she says, "This world is all there is
You can't escape, you hippies."

The flourescent punk female and psychedelic male
Greet at at window
The female, a palely facile freak show
Of affection artificial
And he says, "There's so much more than this world
Just learn to forget, you little girl."

Where you takin' me
Anywhere I'm shakin' free
By the ecstasy surrounding me
If only I choose to lose these blues

Naive Johnson

Tormented by phantoms
And weird, threatening monsters
Symbolic beasts seemed
To give him great trouble
His aggravating problem
Was unrequited love
Naive Johnson was fair game
For connivers with bank rolls
  (Chorus) Robert Johnson knew more than you
            Robert Johnson knew more than you

To a group of Mexican musicians
With a bad case of stage fright
Fresh from the plantation
He wailed into the night
At field studios he sang
Of the fears that gripped him
Of the few things he wanted
From life's constant trap
        Robert Jonhnson knew more than you
        Robert Johnson knew more than you

Entropy

F♯ D C♯

When I held your hand
So long ago
Time took a stand
And refused to go
Our eyes fused
And then we knew
All about each other
All we needed to know
Was that we were together
Arm and arm and no harm
Would ever come
To our love
(Chorus) And I swore our love would never die   A B E
But I also promised I'd never lie   A E D
And I just don't know what to say
God, I wish we'd never had to face this day

Then time started to move
Slow at first but faster
As the magic gazes stagnated
And moved closer to this disaster
But the natural tendency to entropy
Has bled us dry at last
We just can't get past
The past when we vowed
Things could never be
The way that they are now
I don't know how
I just don't know how
To make dead love live again
(Chorus)

LAND OF THE FREE (Jones)

When darkness drops like a bomb come down
To drape a cloak of nothing on this bourgeois town
You and I will find the blind leading the blind
Toward a vain light of freedom from the daily grind
On the corner of a street we'll stand
The storefronts' empty as the faces that understand
Above the gutters and crack houses, the high-rises rise so gra[n]
And this land is their land, this land is our land
   (CHORUS) And in the land of the free
          In the land of the free
          You and I will make a vow
          To make it through somehow

So we embrace like the warmth will erase
The desolation written in the lines on our fac[e]
Lines we learn to recite, a gauntlet thrown at the night
The spirit of life inside for which we figh[t]
And when the day rises like a phoenix from a fire
Of passion and escape and all the night's [d]esires
You and I will see the quiet houses empty
To fill the hungry streets with the brav[e] and the free
        (CHORUS)

Ken Jones

Yuppie Mama

I want a Yuppie Mama
Who ll give me what I need
A place to sleep, food to eat
Me, I ll gladly help her breed
Cute little Yuppie babies
Who ll live happy, happy, happy
Never cold, never hungry
In the Beamer with her and me
          Yuppie Mama, Yuppie Mama

I want a Yuppie Mama
Who ll live to let me play
In the jacuzzi with the VCR
While she works nine to five all day
But I ll treat her right and keep her warm
When her day is done and she comes
To the home she owns in my arms
A house of bliss beyond price
          Yuppie Mama, Yuppie Mama

Ken Jones

Scott -Jones- 89

Her Only Lover Boy

Margarita

When my baby comes to town
All the little boys wanna go down
She got little pink lips and a golden crown
Where all the little boys wanna go down
She pouts; her eyes speak without a sound
And all the little boys wanna go down
To sowseeds of love and reap fields of joy
Down, down, down go all the little boys
    (CHORUS) I wanna be her lover boy
            Her lonely undercover boy

When my baby shakes her hair
All the little boys wanna make her theirs
She shot 'em all down with one of her stares
And all the little boys wanna make her theirs
She tells me none of the others compare
And all the little boys wanna make her theirs
And only I can lay her soul bare
I wanna be her only lover boy there
    (CHORUS)

The Continuing Saga of Capital Bill

Capital Bill smokes a big cigar
Brown-eyed handsome Man drives his car
Capital Bill drives to a high-rise tower
His computers' got numbers, they give him power
 (CHORUS) Middle class Man sweats for a trickle
       Capital Bill owns it all
       But his senseless systems's oh-so fickle
       At least it ain't no hammer and sickle

Capital Bill goes to Vegas to gamble
Just more papers for him to shuffle
Capital Bill owns many mens' sweat
Capital Bill makes ten thousand dollar bets
       (CHORUS)
Capital Bill owns ninety oil wells'
Me, I'm lucky, I afford his fuel
Capital Bill smiles and chucks me a nickle
I'm just a paid extra in his Capital commercial
       (CHORUS)

Scott Jones - 89

UNTIL THE END

It was the 30th day of May
And your folks had gone away
You asked me to come over
Watch T.V. under the covers
~~You told me~~ [I knew right] then and there
~~That would make quite a pair~~ [of the secret world we'd share]
It was then you said with joy
"You'll no longer be a boy"
(CHORUS) And you promised me you'd be my very best friend
You promised me until the very end

It was the 30th day of June
A midsummers afternoon
I kissed you by the river
And swore I saw you shiver
I knew right then and there
That we really cared
It was a moment that made life
Worth trying to live right
(CHORUS)
It was a bleak day in November
I still shake to remember
The day I saw you hand in hand
With another man
I knew right then and there
I longed to touch your golden hair
And drag you to the river
And pull you underwater
(CHORUS)

ACROSS THE GREAT DIVIDE

Uzi shots shatter a gray L.A. day
Three Crips wearing their sacred colors
A young girl shot, home on her way
From visiting her Blood brothers
  (CHORUS) Across the Great Divide
         We hide while they die
         Jaguars and superstars *We've set ourselves up on high*
         And buried children down by the riverside

And the gleaming Beamers of Beverly Hills
Are only a ston'e throw away
But crossing that canyon is sapping the strength
Of a generation slowly fading away
        (CHORUS)

IN BEDTIME EYES

Let's lift the curtain, then let it reveal
You peeking through, so intent to feel
Desperate from desires you both willed and killed
Learning to live your life unfulfilled

From up there on a crystal mantlepiece
To right here in my aching hands
There's a midnight world that lies unfurled
Where we share what we don't understand
        Incendiary mysteries
        Histories in bedtime eyes

YUMMY, YUMMY, YUMMY (LeMaster-Fogle-Jones)

Gonna teach you how to play a new kind of game
You've known it all your life under many different names
Don't worry, baby, if you think you don't know how
I know all the rules, and I think we're alone now
   YUMMY, YUMMMY, YUMMMY, YUMMMY, YUMMMY, YUMMMY
Give me just a minute of your sweet pink lips' time
Stuff I got, baby, gonna blow your mind
I'm a sixty minute man with a lovin' spoonful
Baby, grab my chain and give it a pull
    YUMMY, YUMMY, YUMMY, YUMMY, YUMMY, YUMMY
Yummy, yummy, yummy, got my love in your tummy
Your hands are sticky and your face is gummy
I've got a Big Mac if you're ready for meat
Your cherry pie for desert would be quite a treat
   YUMMY, YUMMY, YUMMY,YUMMY, YUMMY
Crimson and Clover, Sugar, Sugar, and spice
Stuff I got,baby, gonna make you think twice
This ain t no history lesson, ain't no computer file
It's the yummy, yummy, yummy, make the whole world smile
    YUMMY, YUMMY, YUMMMY, YUMMY ,YUMMY

Ken Jones

Michael - Bass
Tennyson: Drums, Scratching
Kyle: Guitar
Ken: Vocals

Bangladesh Babies

Bangladesh babies starving in the street,
Bald heads, bloated bellies, bones for feet.
Hunger in their stomachs, hunger in their eyes,
I like to sit around and watch them die.
Love is such a beautiful thing.

Rich old man in a jute stalk hut,
Farms rice paddies to stuff his gut,
With the month's worth of food he grows in a year,
I like to read about him over pretzels and beer.
Love is such a beautiful thing.

Young boys fish fetid, stagnant pools,
With their own blood as bait, jute stalks as tools,
Adding the catch to the rice to make their diet complete.
I laugh about it as I spit out my meat.
Love is such a beautiful thing.

As the children rise to grab crumbs from the men,
Killer cyclones blow them back down again,
And monsoons come to flood their land.
I think it's funny that they'll never stand.
Love is such a beautiful thing.

If they'd quit reproducing, the death rate would fall.
Why don't we take a knife and sterilize them all?
It's better than reaching a more gruesome end,
I think as I make love to my girlfriend.
Love is such a beautiful thing.

MARY(TRUE LOVE LIES) (Jones)

Mary, have they stolen all your spirit
My baby, I didn't think you'd be like this
My Mary, don't let them beat the heart right out you
  (CHORUS) But I look into your eyes
          And I feel the weight of lies
          And my heart attacks and cries
          For the days of true love ties
          And true love lies

Mary, well, I said I'd be your savior
But baby, for this world there is no cure
So Mary, all I can do is be lovin' pure
          (CHORUS)
Mary, how I long to feel your fingertips
My baby, and to kiss your ruby lips
My Mary, take you on the greatest trip
          (CHORUS)

Ken Jones

Michael: Bass
Tennyson: Drums
Kyle: Acoustic and electric guitars
Ken: Vocals and Keyboard

REMEMBER (Jupp-Jones)

We met in the park after dark
Just to talk, you said
I'll never forget how that long walk
Filled my heart with dread
You told me then and there
That you no longer cared
I couldn't speak, my heart lay bare
All I could do was stare

We wore our care in our eyes
But that style now looks like lies
Heart about to fall off the sleeve
But it beat because it believed
When you whispered to me back then
Always on my mind and forever friends
Did you see the day that your trust
Would disappear into the dust

      Remember--me and you
      Remember--what we used to do
      Remember--you said, "I love you"
      But now you're gone and I'm alone
      Alone

Now a man can only live so long
And belief gives his days meaning
All I dreamed was to lie beside you
With the bad world out of view
But you made me wake and face the day
I could no longer cling to you
For that lesson, I've just got to say
I hate you, but I love you, too

A G E m
O Am x2
G E

[signature: Ken Jones]

Michael Bass
Tennyson Drums & Tambourine
Kyle Lead and Rhythm guitar
Ken Vocals

FURROWED BROWS (LeMaster-Rosenblad-Jones)

A cityscape grays, showing its age
And the waste that threatens to choke it
We vainly pretend to begin's not to end
But the cycle was ours and we broke it
Plastic world makes for atrificial hearts
Mechanical finishes and superficial starts
A culture shaped to help you escape
From the numbing of numbers and Nature's rape
    (CHORUS) Dam your rivers of hate, damn all you know
            Wishes and rituals won't make the pain go

The streets will fill with vibrant life
And an empire;s energy entropies tonight
And you and I go out and see the scattered dots
And pray that in this web of heartlessness we don't get caugh
    (CHORUS)

Ken Jones

Am
Cmaj

G → Am

B7 → F maj; Em

Michael: Bass
Tennyson: Drums
Kyle: Lead and Rhythm Guitar
Ken: Vocals

PARKER GIRL (Jones)

Parker girl, Parker girl,
Great beauty in a terrible world
Parker girl, Parker girl,
Full pink lips and golden curls
Eyes like fire,burn so bright
I long to kiss her in the night
Legs so long, a siren song
I live to protect them from what's wrong

Parker girl, Parker girl
Sensitive sense in a senseless world
Parker girl, Parker girl,
Skin so soft and white as pearls
Eyes like thunder, full of wonder
I long to fill them with my hunger
~~Lips so full, a siren pull~~ Legs so long, a siren song
~~I live to kiss her as my princess girl~~ I live to protect her from what's wrong

Ken Jones

Michael Bass
Tennyson Drums
Kyle: Lead & Rhythm Guitar
Ken Vocals

Heart in the American Empire

```
          Gm                            Cm
     Lonely nights in sweet sheets I dream of you
          Gm                       Eb
     Golden hair as bright as the cityscape's view
          Bbm                   Eb            F
     And like the city those lights are torches
          Gm                    Bbm         F
     Shining beacons on ten thousand front porches
               Dm              Bbm              C
     And in the shadow of the Chevy's and the Porches

                      F
     We stand holding hands
                      Dm    C
     And I beg you to understand
          Bbm               F
     Why I rebel, why I demand
               F5               Eb            F
(Chorus) Some heart in the American Empire
               F5                    Eb
     Some hunger behind the numbers
                  F             F5
     Some passion heat behind the fire
          F5             Eb          F
     Some heart in the American Empire


          Gm                         Cm
     Busy days in hot sheets I dream of you
          Gm                       Eb
     Pale eyes as bright as the cityscape's view
          Bbm                  Eb           F
     And like the city those eyes hold no answers
          Gm                    Bbm        F
     Just burning questions starting to stir
               Dm                Bbm            C
     And in the shadow of the blossoms and the cancers

                      F
     We stand holding hands
                      Dm    C
     And I beg you to understand
          Bbm               F
     Why I rebel, Why I demand
                 (Chorus)
```

Band Schedule - iT is important To keep To This schedule as best we can Please Help. Sooner you set up, sooner ya'll play

(7) - (7.30) Barking Spiders

(7:30) - (8) Barking Spiders Tear Down
Go-Dog-Go Set up

(8) - (8.30) GO-Dog-GO

(8:30) - (9) GO-Dog-GO Tear Down
Peace Corpse set up

(9) Peace Corpse

(9:30) (10) Peace Corpse Tear Down
Nice Strong Arm Set up

(10) Nice Strong Arm

(10:30) - (11) N.S.A. Tear Down

Michael Lawson ⟩ Set up
Tyrant Swing

(11) Michael Lawson

(11:30) Tyrant Swing

(12) - (12:30) Tyrant Swing Tear Down
The Dig set up

(12:30) The Dig
Texas Instruments

(1)

Very important - Have fun

Thanks
Dog

Poets 10 min
Ken Jones before
Tyrant swing
GF Wright before
The Dig

You Thank you Thank you Thank you Thank you Thank you Thank you Thank ya Thank

I'm working on "refreshments" for The Bands

The Way Life Goes

Lyrics

Lyrics with graphics

Flyers

Press

Think of the Kids in Africa

Aren't you gonna finish your dinner
Don't leave all that food for me to throw away
Bloated Negroid babies would give their lives
To have a taste of those fries
  (Chorus) Think of the kids in Africa
            Who don't get the food like you do
            Roamin' the streets of great African cities
            They'd give their lives to be just like you

When population hits the red zone
Then starvation calls a continent home
Starvation is just Nature's Way
Of saying, "My, how you have grown."
            (Chorus)
But you kids today have it so easy
Computer games, Guess jeans, and MTV
Africans still skin animal hides
And they don't have an increase in teen-age suicide
            (Chorus)

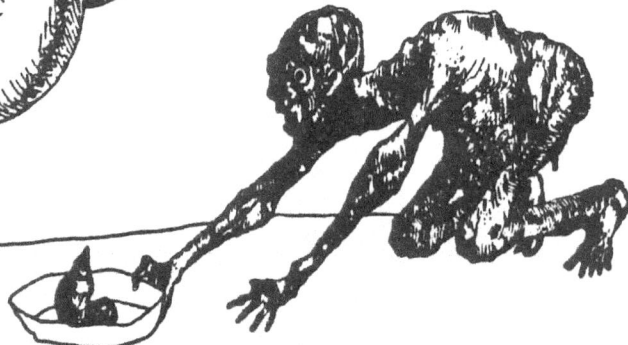

Dog

Dog jumps to the ground
Dog is all around
Dog bites at my leg
Dog wants to make me beg
(Chorus) I'm out walkin' Dog
I'm out talkin' to Dog
He ain't talkin' none to me

Dog,the bitch,begins to itch
Dog itches for fear
Fear of nowhere, fear of here
Dog makes me a wretch
            (Chorus)
Dog is happy, all eyes empty
Dog is fully drained
Of all our pains
Dog is happy, happy, happy, happy
            (Chorus)

ed it shortly
the end of
confirm what
er than had
almost mis-
in England,

g drama of
origins con-
ay: we need
en and why
that Louis
ue to ask is:
imitive pre-
we are? The
y important
decade have
an'. It is the
they give us

called *Homo*
wn as *Homo*
definition of
For a start,
ely unusual
ual features
contains. A
prominent,
forwards as
e are many
ally shaped
er *apparent*
thick hair.
ort so that,
something
in is richly
a ability to

r forelimbs,
degree of
ture of the
brain. No
are useless
erve fibres.
. No other
way that
structured
inside. But
are unique

ts such as
al for their
exchange

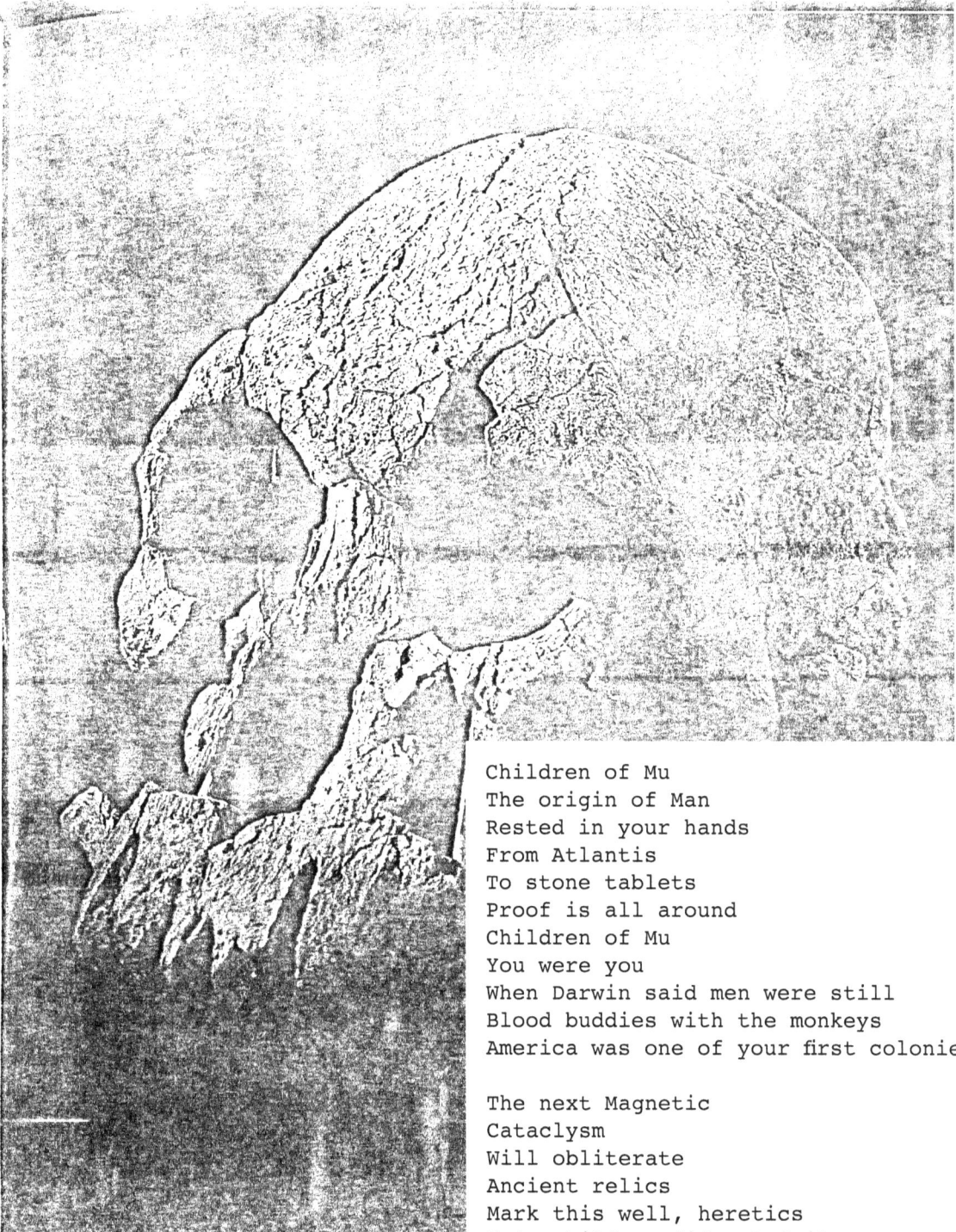

The Great Magnetic Cataclysm
(Children of Mu)

Children of Mu
The origin of Man
Rested in your hands
From Atlantis
To stone tablets
Proof is all around
Children of Mu
You were you
When Darwin said men were still
Blood buddies with the monkeys
America was one of your first colonies.

The next Magnetic
Cataclysm
Will obliterate
Ancient relics
Mark this well, heretics
Mu's children did not fail
The Motherland of all
The Great Civiliations
Mu was quite a nation
When Darwin said men
Were blood buddies with monkeys
America was one of her first colonies.

Find bones of men
And his works' remains
After the last
Magnetic Cataclysm
Children of Mu
The origin of Man
Is out of your hands.

LIVING IN A BOURGEOIS TOWN—PEACE CORPS

LIVING IN A BOURGEOIS TOWN
PEACE CORPS

1.THE FIDELITY EMPLOYEE 2.BOURGEOIS BLUES 3.PARTYING FRANK 4.THE ALIEN 5.PASTURES OF PLENTY 6.CONSUMPTION BLUES 7.OCCUPIED AMERICA 8.YOUR BRIGHT SMILE 9.MENAGE A TROIS

PEACE CORPS is:

Rob Cooley-Drums, Percussion, Backing Vocals
Mitch Ginsburg-Bass, Guitar
Gene Huang-Guitar, Bass, Violin
Ken Jones-Vocals, Backing Vocals
Steve Vague-Saxophones, Backing Vocals

SIDE ONE

THE FIDELITY EMPLOYEE

Every day I smile at a thousand clean white faces
When they come to this place to check their balances
In my three-piece suit and tie, I'm decked out to the nines
When folks ask me how I'm doin', I just answer 'Fine'
(CHORUS) I'm an employee of Fidelity
            This glass tower's security

Some days I dream of bein' its president
Then these glass towers don't seem so heaven sent
So when I climb in my comfort chariot
The black landscape don't seem so desolate
            (CHORUS)
Every night at home a few brews calm me down
Spend my time just flipping those channels around
From my couch one box controls the world
All I need now is a pretty little girl
Then I'll have my security
As an employee of Fidelity

BOURGEOIS BLUES

Well, he's a bourgeois man
Living in a bourgeois town
Neat streets greet his gaze
Nothing here gets him down
Miles of manicured ground
Stretch to the horizon
Not a spot left open
'Cause nothing here gets him down
(CHORUS) Nothing here gets him down (3)
              Nothing here gets him down (3)

Well, your toil on the soil
And your sweat in the steel mill
Your hot breath mechanically
Moving to lay a brick
Laid him like a saved baby
In this protected niche
A clean American room
In a bourgeois town

   (CHORUS)

PARTYING FRANK

With my B.M.W. in park
I light out for the party in the dark
With my Ray-bans and button down shirt
I look like I'd never play in dirt
My daddy's rich, too
He could buy and sell you
Like you were candy hearts
Inside the shopping cart
(CHORUS) Cause I'm a Partying Frank

Parties like this with terrific friends
And I always party to the party's end
It's a blast to be in fraternities
With all these extracurricular activities
Drank two bottles
Straight Mexican tequila
Watch out below
Watch me blow

MENAGE A TROIS

Let me tell you about my menage a trois
Met two girls in a local bar
Took 'em out to the make-out park
Slipped 'em my sausage in their daddy's car
Menage a Trois

It was Long Tall Sally and Suzie Q
Together they mixed a twitchin' brew
What a graphic, Sapphic couple
Ripplin' the tips of their nipples
Menage a Trois

One stripped before me as the other grinned
Her upraised leg begged me to stick it in
It's been so long since she's felt a man
Her moans echoed like it was the Grand Canyon
Menage a Trois

ALL LYRICS BY KEN JONES
ALL MUSIC BY PEACE CORPS

Recorded at Lone Star Recording Studios
Engineered by Michael Fogle
Copyright 1988 Peace Corps

1.THE FIDELITY EMPLOYEE 2.BOURGEOIS BLUES 3.PARTYING FRANK
4.THE ALIEN 5.PASTURES OF PLENTY 6.CONSUMPTION BLUES
7.OCCUPIED AMERICA 8.YOUR BRIGHT SMILE 9.MENAGE A TROIS

DEAR PERSONS:

I CURRENTLY TEACH COURSES IN POPULAR CULTURE AND THE
MEDIA USING A WIDE VARIETY OF CLASSIC AND CONTEMPORARY
RESOURCES. AS CAPTAIN MEDIA, I ALSO PRODUCE AND
BROADCAST RADIO SPECIALS THAT FEATURE QUALITY AUDIO
ITEMS RARELY HEARD ELSEWHERE. MY PURPOSE IS TO
ACQUAINT STUDENTS AND LISTENERS WITH DIVERSE CULTURAL
MATERIALS WHILE PROVIDING RECOMMENDATIONS. IN THIS
REGARD I'D SINCERELY APPRECIATE A SAMPLE COPY OF
KEN JONES AND THE PEACE CORPS

THANK YOU,

BEN PRICE
PSYCHOLOGY DEPT.
SAN JOSE CITY COLLEGE
2100 MOORPARK AVE.
SAN JOSE, CA. 95128

"RECOMMENDED MEDIA"
BROADCASTS ON

Airchecks Radio

MEMBER AUDIO INDEPENDENTS

```
THE CLOCK DROOPS

Gazing up at the bloated sky
Filled with planes that swiftly fly
Through the tears your God cries
Our clock ticks -- we no not why

Down below, why bother to try
No place to hide that still is dry
Rivers of blood and rise
No tears drip from my eyes

Flaked-skinned children litter camp
The holy ground soaked bloody damp
Death is king, and still the champ
The clock spins and dims the lamp

Candy for the kids makes them smile
Look at them lie in the latest style
Playing corpus delecti is fun for a while
Till their blood puddles with acid and bile

Jesus loves the little children
All the little children of this world
Jesus loves you little children
He set your clock stuck in this world

                              KEN JONES
```

AN ORDINARY DOG IN AMERICA EATS BETTER THAN SHE DOES.

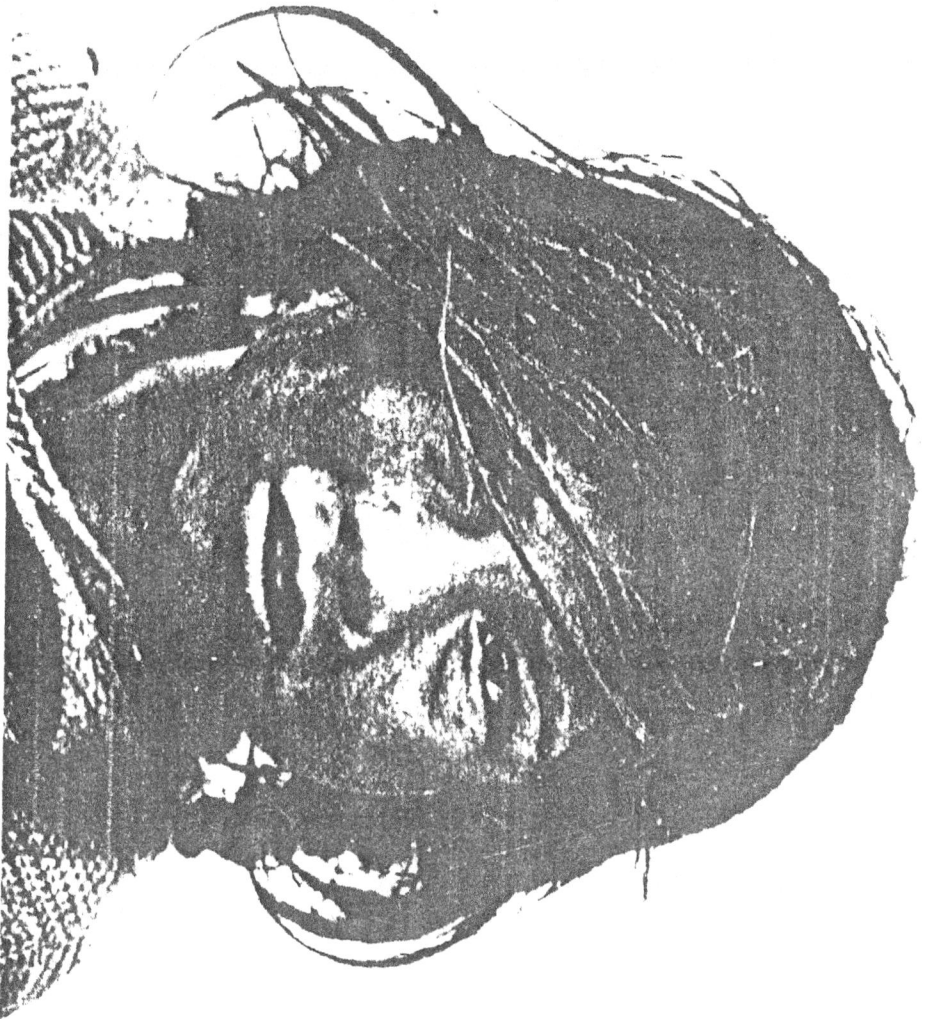

Our Concerns

Children of war
Crowd into pigpens
Wounds open and sore
Only their lives to defend
On beds of suffering
Limbs lost and deformed
Bullets poetry singing
To bring even more harm
But what do we care, what can we do
This bullshit doesn't concern me and you

They cross the barbed wire
To try and escape
But the soldiers yell "Fire!"
And their bodies are raped
By the black bits of metal
That moan in the air
And tear into their skulls
Laying gray matter bare
But what do we care, what can we do
This bullshit doesn't concern me and you

They make the long trek
Across the dead land
Their country as wrecked
As the stumps of their hands
Their journey so noble
Like the long march of Mao
The government's are bulls
The children raped, bleeding cows
But what do we care, what can we do
This bullshit doesn't concern me and you

THEY'RE NOT DANCING IN DETROIT

The Way Life Goes

Broken window looking out
On whitewashed golden towers
She reclines on a black-faced mattress
And sniffs her dying flowers
Waiting for the phone to ring
With another broken promise it brings
She now knows the way life goes
She answers it no more

Inside the tower the great men sit
In chairs of outback leather
They discuss Wall Street stocks
Their daughters, wives, the weather
Still locked in armors of fear
Bolted masks of steely cheer
They now know the way life goes
They treasure it no more

Molasses streams of people pass
Flowing toward a point
The greatest of Man's achievements
Can't knock these lines out of joint
Vertical cliffs rise high in the air
And disappear into nothing
They now know the way life goes
No one cares about anything anymore
No more

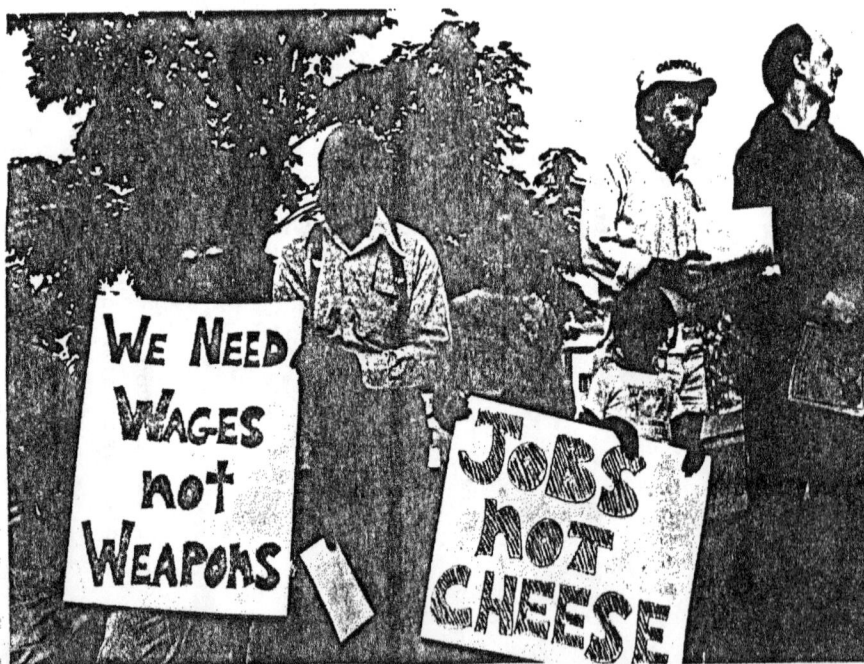

WE NEED WAGES not WEAPONS

JOBS not CHEESE

Released 1987

PEACE CORPS

YUPPIE POSTER CHILD

1. DRESS CODE 2. PASTURES OF PLENTY 3. A TASTE OF THE WILD 4. THE BLIND CHILD 5. BIRTH DEFECT 6. IN A COCKED RIFLE'S CRACK 7.WATCH HER SQUAT 8.CALL ME JOHN HENRY 9.GOD BLESSED AMERICA 10.DOG 11. THEPINNACLE TO THE PANHANDLE 12. THINK OF THE KIDS IN AFRICA 13. MEMPHIS, TENNESSEE 14. WISHES FOR THE SIXTIES.

All Lyrics by Ken Jones
All Music by Peace Corps
Peace Corps Is:

Rob Cooley- Drums, Backing Vocals
Mitch Ginsburg- Bass, Guitar
Gene Huang Guitar, Bass , Violin
Ken Jones- Vocals, Backing Vocals
Steve Vague- Saxophone

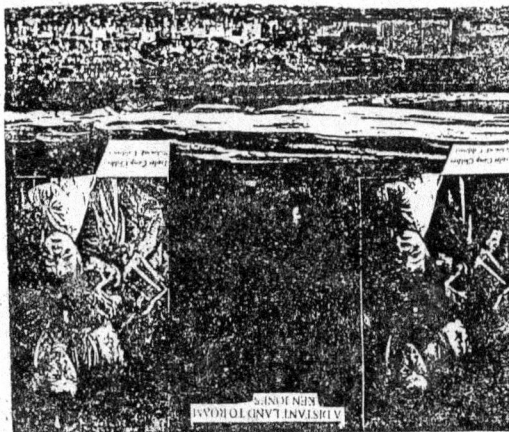

A DISTANT LAND TO ROAM
KEN JONES

1. A DISTANT LAND TO ROAM 2.THE ALIEN 3. SHARE THE NIGHTMARE 4. SONG TO JIMMIE 5.WIDE BEAUTIFUL EYES 6. TRACES OF NATURE 7. OCCUPIED AMERICA 8. LIVE TO DIE 9. I DON'T BELONG 10. LAST CALL AT THE LOST CALL 11. SOMEDAY NEVER COMES 12. PEACE

LAND OF NO PURPOSE
KEN JONES

1.The Bridge2.The Peace Corps Reader3.Rave On4.Love
5.Dreams of Heaven6.Desperate to Feel7.She Breathes
To Me8.Smorgasbord

Musicians:
Mike Alvarez: Acoustic and slide guitar on 1, Drums
Mitch Ginsburg: Acoustic guitar on 2,3 ; bass on 5,6
Ken Jones: Vocals on all tracks; piano on 4
Byron Scott: Acoustic guitar on 5,6,7,8
          ALL LYRICS BY KEN JONES
          ENGINEERED BY MIKE ALVAREZ
          COPYRIGHT 1988 KEN JONES
     THE BRIDGE (Alvarez-Jones)

     We drove across
     This steel strait-jacket
     As I gripped the upholstery
     And the city lights beneath
     Twinkled like Christmas tinsel
     In a firmament sprinkled with spots
     Of incomprehensible wonder
     A city's fiery hunger
      (CHORUS) The Bridge, The Bridge
               Beneath the Seeds of Man
               Hard river runs
               Between father and son
     Now things are so unstable
     Nothing to hold onto
     Except the strength of two together
     When the weary day is through

GLITCH
SAMPLER #4
"TEXAS - THE MUSICAL MELTING POT"
MEET THE BANDS + BUY OUR RECORD + GET AUTOGRAPHS
RECORD RELEASE
PARTY
at ANTONE'S
RECORD STORE
2928 GUADALUPE STREET
FRI DEC 9th 5-8pm
FREE BEER LIVE MUSIC

the wartime Manhattan Project

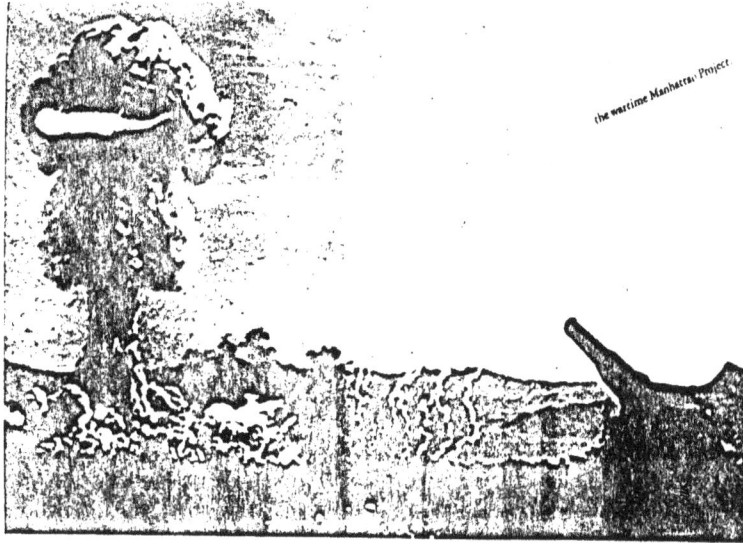

Figure 9.12 The first live nuclear artillery test, **Shot Grable**, on 25 May, 1953. A 280mm nuclear artillery shell with an explosive yield of 15 k was exploded in an airburst over the Nevada Test Site.

k-12A) missiles active (198

57 missile production deli

Number Deployed:

fixed 25 + m underground
hardened silo with missile sus-
pension, shock isolated floor,

Strategic Bomber Force
B-52 STRATOFORTRESS

Long-range, heavy bomber used by the Strategic Air Command. Presently deployed and modified into three versions: B-52D, G, and H.

HONEST JOHN rockets

Manhattan Project

Sea-Based Missile Systems
POSEIDON Submarine

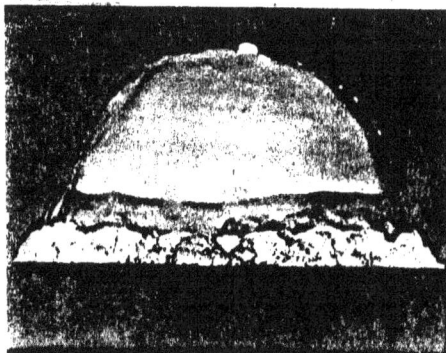

he fireball of the world's first nuclear explosion, Trinity test-site, Alamogordo, 0.034 seconds

They said it couldn't happen here
After all, we've always lived in fear
The winds blew hot, then grew cold
When skin didn't melt, it froze
Can't stumble from this sterile place
It doesn't have a human face
I'm living in nuclear winter
But I remember what they said
Before we went under
Duck and cover!
Duck and cover!

On the wall, a silhouette
Screams a silent pirouette
Above ground, the starving packs
Prime for a primal attack
But, Thank God, I've got my gun
Can't live now without a weapon
I'm living in nuclear winter
But I remember what they said
Before we went under
Duck and cover!
Duck and cover!

Let the four winds blow!
Let my bald skull glow!
Annihilate and celebrate
This nuclear winter is great!

DEPLOYMENT:
Launch Platform:

CONTRACTORS: Boeing Aerospace Company
Seattle, WA; Wichita, KS
(prime)
Pratt & Whitney
(engines)
Boeing Witchita
(offensive avionics)
IBM
(navigation and weapons delivery computer)

The Way Life Goes

PART ONE

Lyrics

Lyrics with graphics

Flyers

Press

'Waiting for something to happen???

Tim Fry, 17, is a junior in high school at Village Christian School in Sun Valley, California, where he was born and raised. After graduation, he plans to go to a trade school and learn an occupation.

Tim wants to go on to a trade school to learn about heavy-duty mechanics.

'The sound of

WARNING!

BEFORE
AFTER

PEACE CORPSE
PEACE CORPSE

Hardcore
Punk-
1985-86

Graphics by
Jerry Dog
for
Flying
Horse
Zine
1985-86

BLACK CAT LOUNGE

FREE ADMISSION

8:30 pm

THURS. 29th

THE SURGEON GENERAL HAS BEEN CONDUCTING EXPIRIMENTS WITH THE BAND PEACE CORPSE. LISTENING TO THE BAND HAS BEEN ___ WITH CONVULSIONS, MUTATIONS, AND CANCER OF THE COLON.

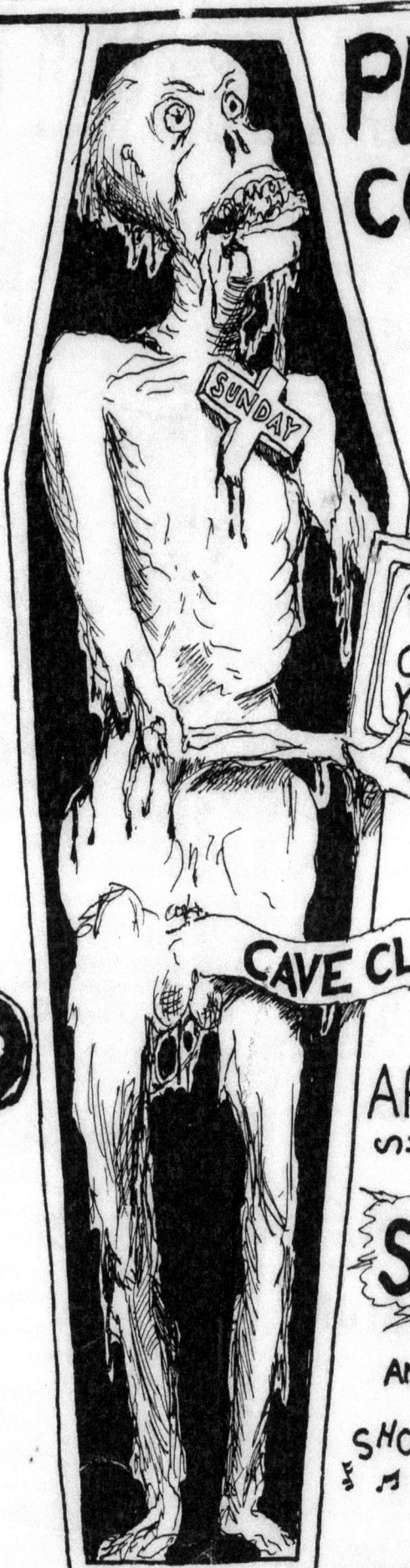

PEACECORPSE

PEACE CORPSE

SUNDAY

TECHNI-
COLOR
YAWNS

CAVE CLUB

APRIL 12TH
SUNDAY

STORM

AND THE

SHOCK TROOPERS

FLYING Horse

u-men

the Blood Sucking Godevils

the DIου

JOEY G

Symposium

ken jones

WARD 69-86

chuc and whammo

June

FANCY

PEACE CORP.

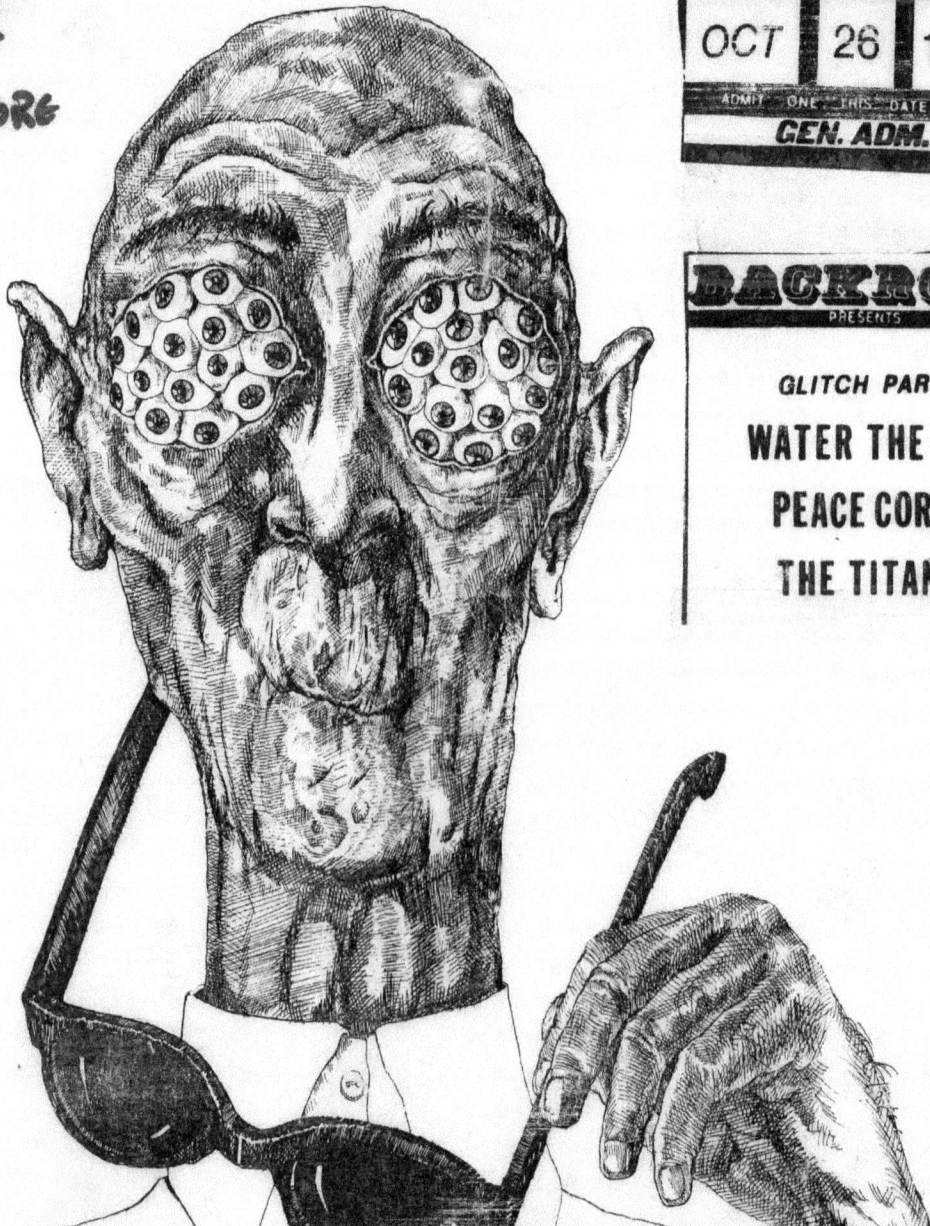

FREE PASS
PRICE

AVAILABLE
AT YOUR
LOCAL
RECORD STORE

BACK ROOM

MO	DAY	YEAR
OCT	26	1988

ADMIT ONE THIS DATE
GEN. ADM.

BACKROOM
PRESENTS

GLITCH PARTY

WATER THE DOG

PEACE CORPS

THE TITANS

NIKKI, JOIN THE PEACE CORPS

Khrushchev and Kennedy, Vienna, 1961: a "world of diversity

A "WORLD OF DIVERSITY"

AT: "THE RITZ" FAJITA FLATS
WED. w/ BEER SAT. July 18
July 15 NUTS w/ Guardez LOU

THE FUTURE OF LAW ENFORCEMENT.

This Time
It's Personal.

Full Metal
PARTY

SATURDAY

July **25**

3215 DANCY

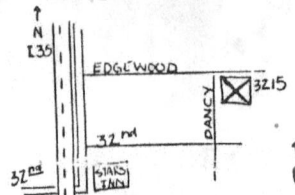

LIVE
MUSIC...

with

BEAST
OF
EDEN

★★★★

9:00 PM

ALVARO
CHRIS
HOLLY
JONNATHAN
KAYLA
RAY
BUCK
TRACY
VANDY
EDDIE

FLYING HORSE SYMPOSIUM

MUSIC BY.
DO-DAT
BAD
 MUTHA
  GOOSE
OBOYO
NEON
 LEON
ROOSTER
 DANIEL
(Premier)
Wardshock
 The
 Movie
PoeTry By:
G.F.
 WrighT
Ken Jones
SaT
March
 29 @
BEACH
9 P.M.
Til ?

PC

DOWN WITH RACISM FROM BOSTON TO SOUTH AFRICA!

JOIN...
THE PEACE CORPS
At: Fajta Flats
Sat. Sept 19 @ 9:

CELEBRATING OUR GOLDEN ANNIVERSARI

WE WUV YOU WILLWEE!

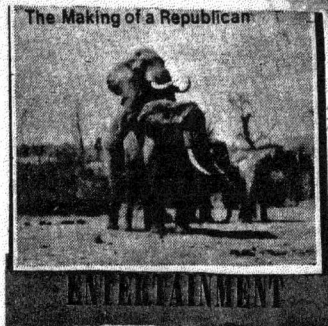

FLASH

The Making of a Republican

ENTERTAINMENT

Now "You" Can Have A High Time!

Nov. 25th at

Experience the Tripp!!

Liberty Lunch
477-046L
405 W. 2nd at Guadalupe

"IGNORANCE OF THE LAW IS NO EXCUSE."

Know whom you're dealing with

THE MAIN COURSE

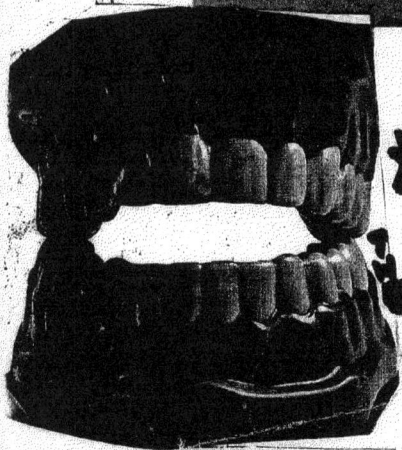

MIKE ALVAREZ BAN
WITH SPECIAL GUESTS
PLUS:
POCKET FISHERMEN
HEATHER! $4
THE WEEDS
KEN JONES
SPECIAL EFFECTS
AT THE DOOR

FEEL HAPPY TAKE A DRUG YOU DON'T REALLY UNDERSTAND

Trippy Tip
Did you ever notice that Shower to Shower body powder doesn't stick when you're tripping? -
—Susan and Jory, Chicago, Ill.

COMPILED BY W. T. W. INC

STEP CHILD FOR
PRODUCTIONS '84

FLYING HORSE #11
KEN JONES, D.
JEWEL— poetry

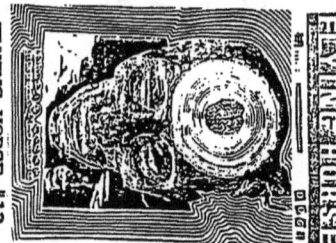

FLYING HORSE #12
RANDY "BISCUIT"
TURNER— cover
KEN JONES, JUNE

FLYING HORSE #6 & #7
both in one volume— ASH
RANDY TURNER, I.K BRUNEL
STRAPPADOS interview

FLYING HORSE #1
poetry by G.F.
WRIGHT.
cartoons by
BILL BARMINSKI

FLYING HORSE #2
poetry-G.F.
WRIGHT.
giant ELVIS
poster

FLYING HORSE #8
poetry— KEN JONES
G.F. WRIGHT
ASH, ERIC TOOLEY

FLYING HORSE #3
this issue
passed out at
WOODSHOCK 85'

FLYING HORSE #4
JUKE BOX cover
G.F. WRIGHT
DANIEL JOHNSTON

FLYING HORSE #9
G.F. WRIGHT, KEN
JONES, RANDY TURNER
DANIEL JOHNSTON

FLYING HORSE #5
poetry— KEN JONES
drawings— I.K.
BRUNEL.

FLYING HORSE #10
poetry— LIZ BELILE,
KEN JONES
IDEALS interview

A NEW TAPE FROM

PEACE

CORPS

LIVING IN A BOURGEOIS TOWN

photos by David L. Wilson

AT: INNER SANCTUM
SOUND EXCHANGE
WATERLOO

Released 1987

YUPPIE POSTER CHILD
PEACE CORPS

YUPPIE POSTER CHILD
PEACE CORPS

YUPPIE POSTER CHILD
PEACE CORPS

YUPPIE POSTER CHILD
PEACE CORPS

YUPPIE POSTER CHILD
PEACE CORPS

PEACE CORPS
YUPPIE POSTER CHILD

PEACE CORPS
YUPPIE POSTER CHILD

LITCH SAMPLER 4

EXAS THE MUSICAL MELTING POT

GLITCH SAMPLER-4
Texas-The Musical Melting Pot

Photo by Al Breitenbach

uring Los Deflectors, the European Sex Machine, Johnny Law, the

well, might as well Join the
PEACE CORPS

FRI. OCT. 23

With
BLOODSUCKING
GO-DEVILS
and
the IDEALS

FRIDAY
OCTOBER 23
10 p.m. - 2 a.m.
at the

RITZ

Theatre
6th

OCTOBER 1987 $2.50

Bulletin
of the Atomic Scientists

Canadian
Defense Debate

JOIN PEACE THE CORPS

PEACE CORPS PEACE CORPS

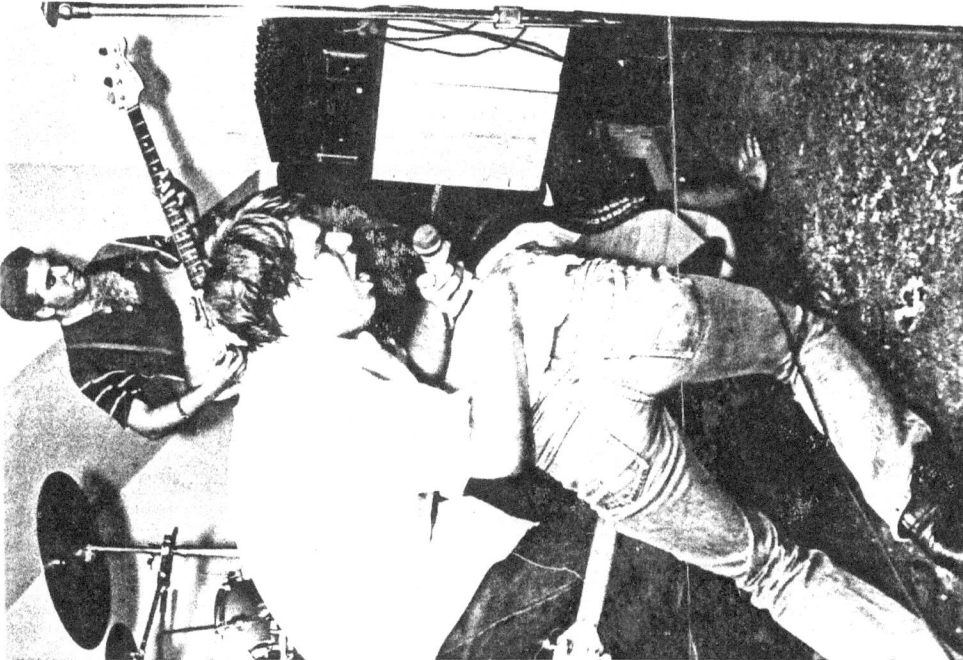

...ke to thank the Austin Chronicle,
...esman, the Daily Texan, Fatalist
...¶ 37, David Wilson for the front
...bs we've played: The Ritz, Steamboat,
..., Fajita Flats, the Loft, Liberty
...e Beach RIP and the Continental Club
...who've checked us out and enjoyed

Jim delivers his letters on foot. It takes him five hours to complete his route.

Join the

PEACE CORPS

When I'm not playing sports, I have an after-school job, working on truck engines. I get paid $4.50 an hour. I have a knack for mechanical work. I enjoy working on engines. I first became interested in it a few years ago, when my father was a drag-race-boat driver. He let me work on his boat, and since then I've been working on every engine I can find. Gaining experience when you're young is important. But to be a good mechanic, you've got to have it in your blood.

at

This is a respected job. When I ha my uniform on and my mailbag on shoulder, I'm a representative of the U government. Most people like me.

Big

MAMOU

Wednesday Dec. 30
10 p.m.

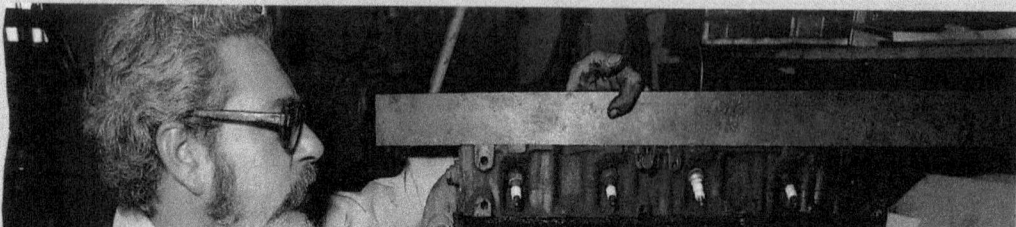

PEACE CORPSE

SATURDAY, MAY 17

BEACH

9:00 PM

'The worker shoulders the burden'

Manny Gleicher, 55, has been in the accounting business for 20 years. He graduated from Syracuse University and New York Law School, and attended special accounting classes before opening his accounting business.

A moment of light relief during a busy day's shooting on location.

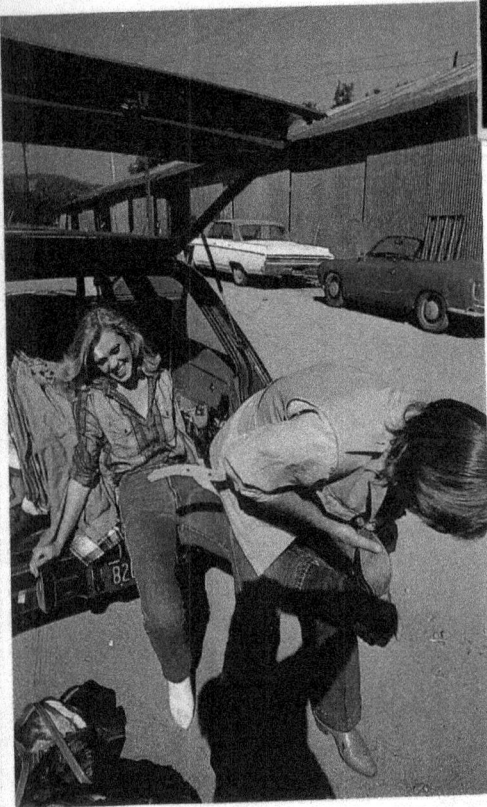

PEACE CORPS & DO DAT'

THE

RED DRAGON (RitZ)

W_D.   THE 9th - RELIEF AFTER A HARD DAY'S

'It's not easy   WORK

"What civilized humankind is
a thirst for BEER!"
— L.M. Boyd —

PEACE CORPSE will play at 10:30.

"I wanna Par-ar-tee!"
— Big Boys —

Aug 7

At Mamie & Jessica's

...kkeg 2005 Beaird 805...

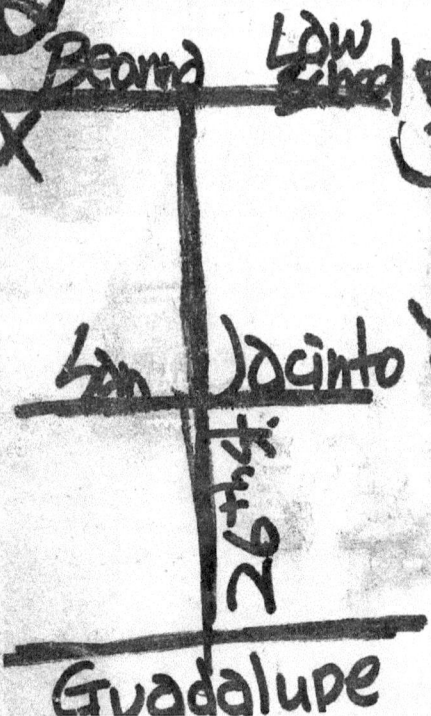

Beaird   Law
                School

San Jacinto   26 July

Guadalupe

The Peace Corps e

&

DO DAT

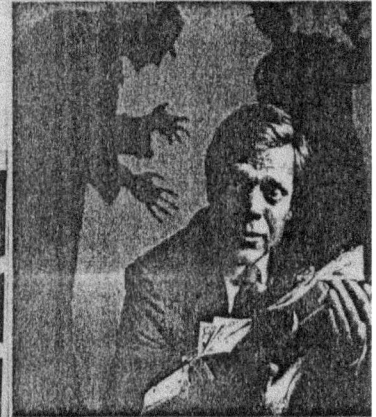

small $

Vietnam tour packages
offered by companies
Itineraries usually include other Asian cities

Fresh pastures at

THE

RITZ

FRIDAY SEPT. 4TH

south by southwest

SXSW II

music and media conference

SXSW MUSIC FESTIVAL

THURSDAY, MARCH 10	MUSIC FESTIVAL PASS
SATURDAY, MARCH 12	GOOD FOR ADMISSION
SUNDAY, MARCH 13	TO ALL THESE SHOWS

All shows 9-2am Thu & Sun, 8-2am Sat. unless otherwise noted

Also good for Back Room 1 & 2, Friday, March 11

All artists subject to change ★ Acts listed in order of appearance

★ THE AUSTIN ★

CHRONICL

PEACE CORPS
Austin, TX

south by southwest

SXSW II

the second media conference

Musicians Regi

Peace Corps Tape Release Party!!

"Living in a Bourgeois Town"

at Inner Sanctum
504 W. 24th

Shiner beer

Friday, March 11
5:00 P.M.
Live set at 5:30

see Peace Corps at SXSW at the Loft
Sunday, March 13

Peace Corp.

Multi-national musical conglomeration. Manu factures full-throttle psychedelic funk/rock with radical proselytizing poetics. Formerly Peace Corps, now reformed in a merge with God's lea guitarist Byron "Siren" Scott, Greg Psycho-Hip drummer, bassist Mitch Ginsburg, vocalist/lyric Ken Jones.

Discography: "In a Cocked Rifle's Crack," tra on *4th Glitch Sampler; Living in a Bourgeois To Yuppie Poster Child*, local cassettes; *A Distant Land to Roam, Land of No Purpose* (produced b Mike Alvarez), Ken Jones solo acoustic tapes.

1987 Austir Recordings

TAPES

KEN JONES
A DISTANT LAND TO ROAM

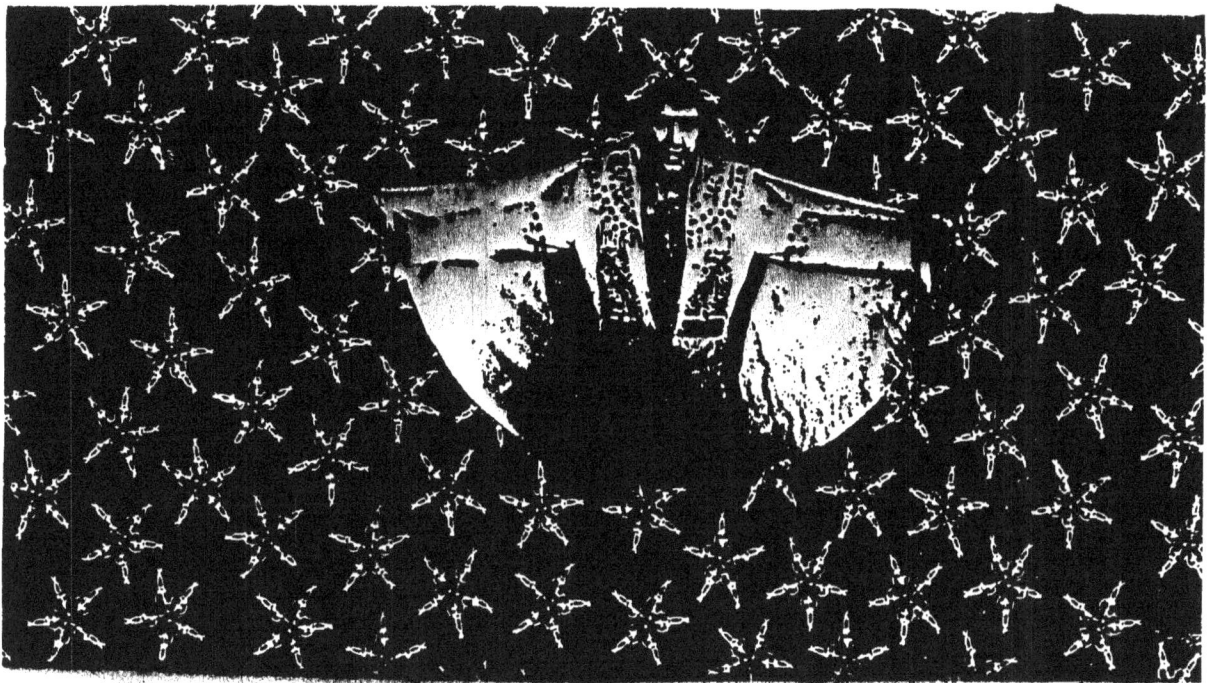

MUXIK BX:

POISON

DANIEL JONSTON

PEZ

Speci
ELVI
SHRI
BY
CONTR
RAT

Sep
2

Toshio Hirano

P#ETRY BX:
RANDY BISCUIT
TURNER
G. F. ucking "A
WRIGHT
KEN TOO TIGHT
JONES

AN THIS
AND MORE!!
IN THE 1"
FLYING
HORSE
SYMPOSIUM

STARTS
SHOW 8 PM

AT THE BEACH
CABARET

SAT.
May 3rd, AT 6:00 PM

...kers United Will Never Be Defeated
... celebrate Mayday (The International Worker's Day)

Beer, Insanity, politics, beastly
-ness

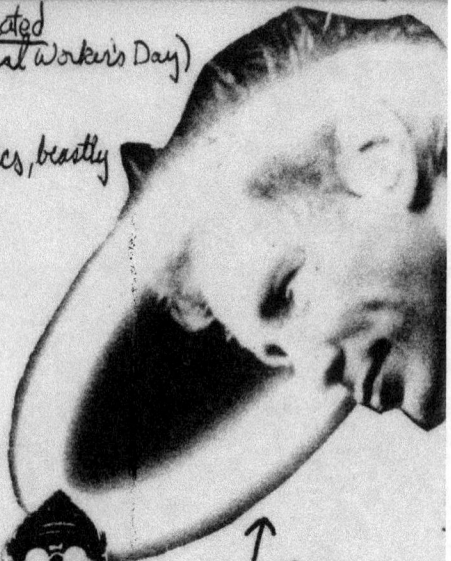

↑
(god)

THE NEW Guild CO-OP
510 W. 23rd St.
(At Nueces)

Presents ~~&~~ the

MAYDAY PARTY!!!

Come Early! - Bands Start at 5:00 PM
+ Beer

TEXAS INSTRUMENTS

CHEAP THRILLS

GUARDEZ LOU
HUNDREDTH MONKEY
PEACE CORPSE
MINUS GRACE
FURNITURE
TOMMY BOYKIN
and the
CHAUVINISTS
HOMEBOYS
MISSING LINK

MAYDAY! MAYDAY!!!

FEAR NOTHING

The Rev. Jerry Falwell
THE BEAST
666

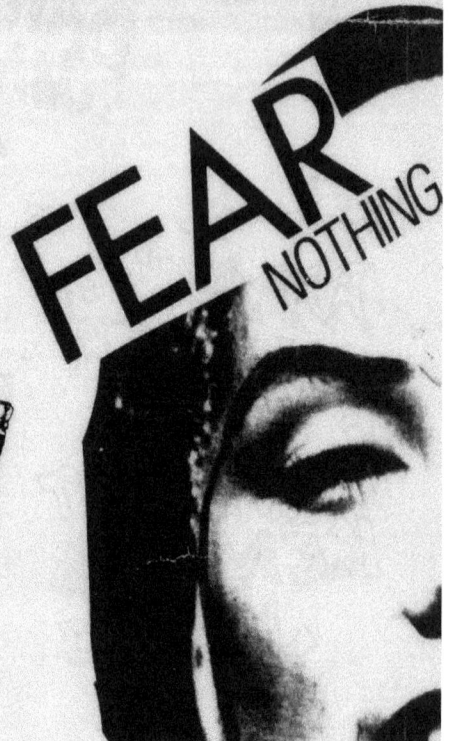

APPLE, BRAIN + BULLET TOUR

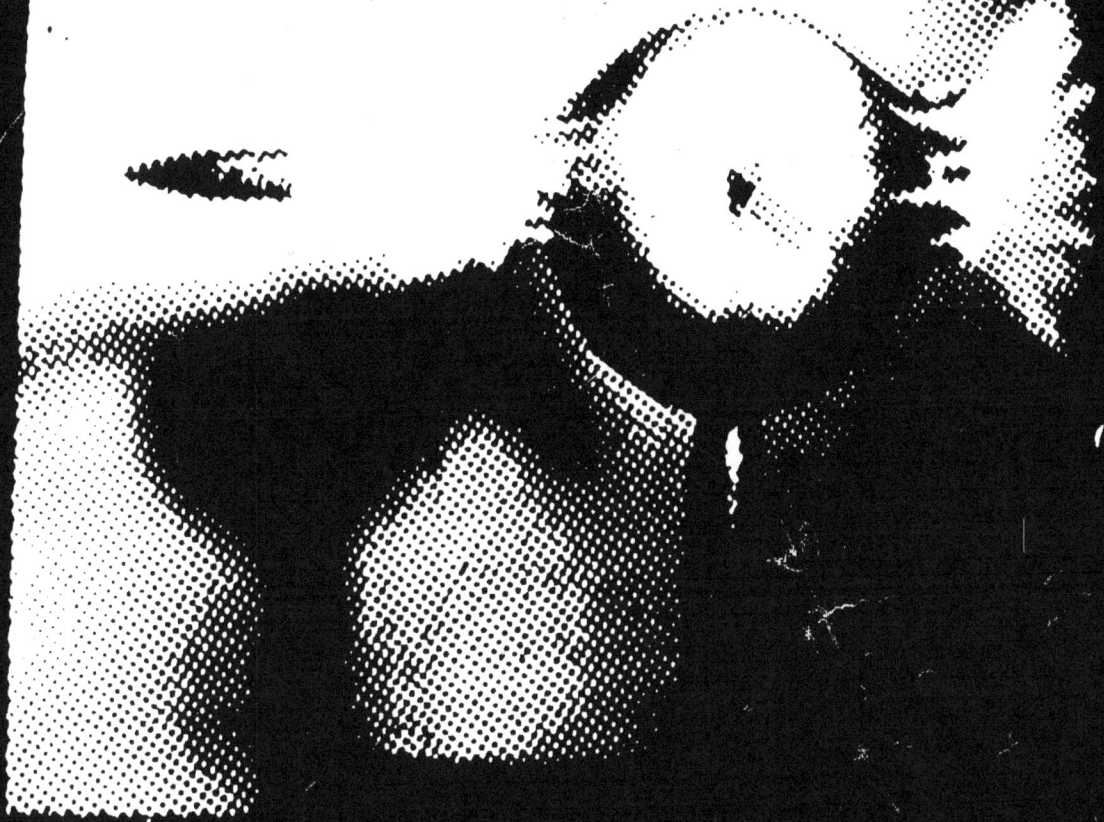

PEACE
THE CORP.
GO DEVILS

SAT. MAY 17th   BENIFIT FOR HUNGRY WOLFE   STARTS 7pm

THE DIG

NICE STROUNG ARM

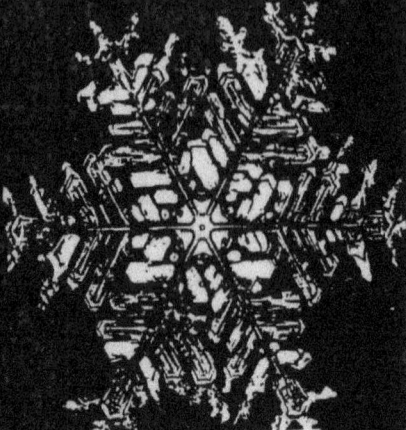

MICHAEL LAWSON

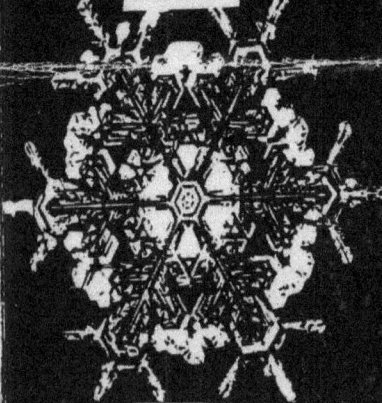

GO-DOG-GO

TEXAS INTRUMENTS

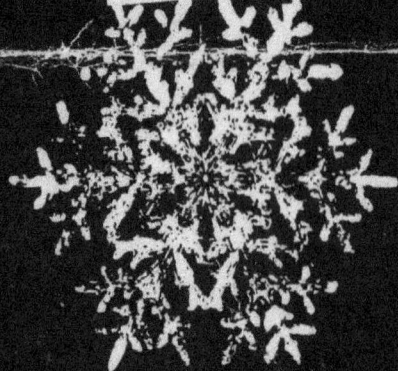

PEACE CORPSE

TYRANT SWING

BARKING SPIDERS

G.F.WRIGHT

?????YOU???????

KEN JONES

Peace Corps
AT THE
LOFT

see Peace Corps at SXSW at the Loft
Sunday, March 13

Peace Corps Tape Release Party!!
"Living in a Bourgeois Town"
at Inner Sanctum
504 W. 24th

Shiner Beer

Friday, March 11
5:00 P.M.
Live set at 5:30
see Peace Corps at SXSW at the Loft
Sunday, March 13

IF You See
Louie Benueve

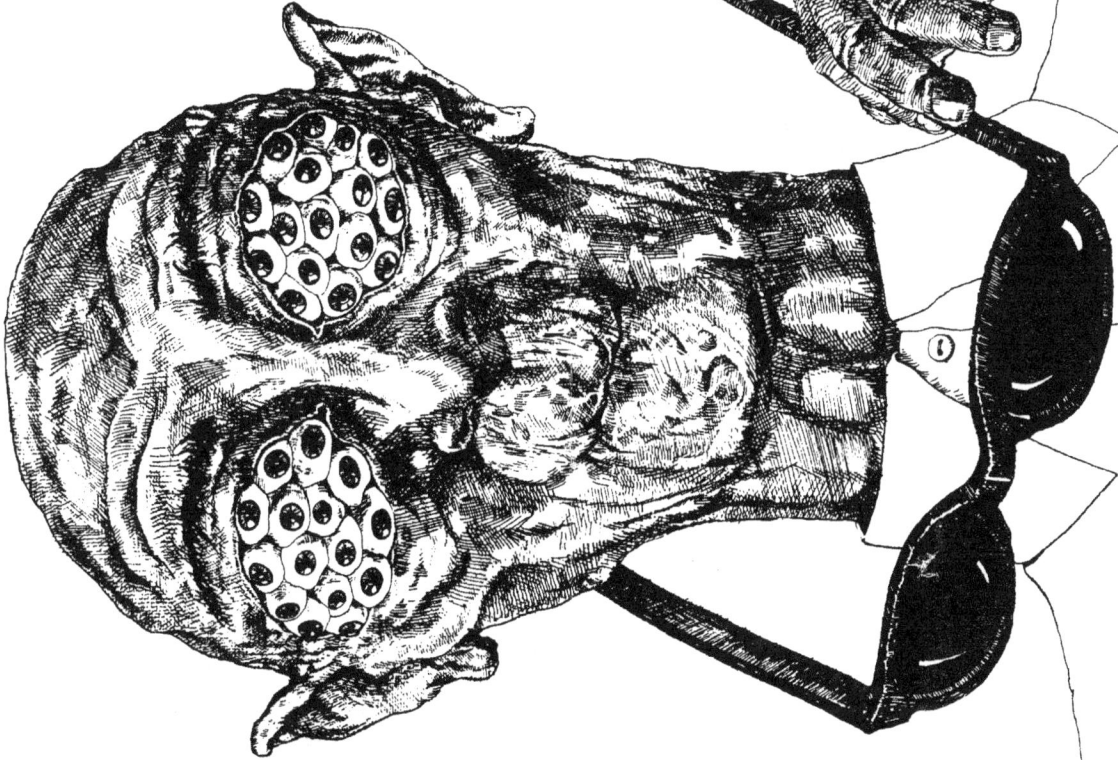

BACK ROOM

PRICE

GOOD FOR ONE FREE ADMISSION FOR ANYONE 21 OR OVER

THE TITANS
PEACE CORPS
WATER THE DOG
GLITCH PARTY

MO OCT
DAY 26
YEAR 1988

ADMIT ONE THIS DATE

GEN. ADM.

BACKROOM PRESENTS

FLYING HORSE
FLYING HORSE
FLYING HORSE
FLYING HORSE
FLYING HORSE
FLYING HORSE

CATHERINE THE GREAT ISSUE

BEACH CABARET

FLYING HORSE SYMPOSIUM

SCRATCH ACID
THE IDEALS
TYRANT SWING
BRUCE

PERSONS WITH
PINK UNDIES
$1 OFF

POETRY BY
LIZ B.
KEN JONES?
?????????

SAT, JUNE 14th

CAT-COUNTY JAIL
criminal # KITTY

The Way Life Goes

PART ONE

Lyrics

Lyrics with graphics

Flyers

Press

PEACE CORPS
Yuppie Poster Child

Peace Corps is Rob Cooley-drums, backing vocals, Mitch Ginsburg-bass, guitar Gene Huang-guitar, bass, Violin Ken Jones-vocals, backing vocals Steve Vague-Saxophone. This tape was engineered by Kyle Rosenblad, with very humorous cover art by Rob Cooley and DOG. These guys have been around a couple of years now, they released a very hardcore/political tape last year that got rave reviews in Maximum Rock'n'roll etc.
They have veered away from hardcore to a more accessible funky, rock'n'roll sound with horns etc.

Side A begins w/ DRESS CODE:"Abutton down shirt for men, neatly tucked in, skirts showing a little skin are fine for women, and high-heeled shoes to torture your toes, We enforce a strict dress code." I witnessed these guys break into a snarling version of DRESS CODE at the RITZ after some drunken/nazi/frat boys happened to stumble in, they seemed very confused. PASTURES OF PLENTY:Nice poppy tune,political lyrics. "And the backs of the millions creaked and echoed with pain to make these playland streets seem pristine and sane." THE BLIND CHILD:Sounds like R.E.M.... "We're just killing time, bend the mind of the blind child." BIRTH DEFECT:Great hardcore tune. "I came out hungry and knowing nothing, A passionate moment's accident, I grew up quiet but knowing something, Ugly lingered under the oxygen tent, Half in love with easeful Death, But grasping for every gasping breath, I saw so much to reject, I guess it's just a birth defect." IN A COCKED RIFLE'S CRACK:Good hard rocker, "I'm holding on to the storm's wet kiss, I'm holding on tight like this, On a candle's smooth back, the flame a shaman's mantra chanted in a fight against eternal fright, outside atmospheric torment,an ominous portent." WATCH HER SQUAT:Swell little ditty w/ great lead sax and the lyrics;"I want to watch her squat, it gets me really hot, and when I see her pee, it sends shivers right through me, her scars are desire's angels, I live for a shot of her snot, to play fully fluff her dandruff, then watch her squat, her urine sweet sweet syrup to me, I accept the waste of her body as necessary for her beauty." They even do a cover of GOD BLESSED AMERICA by Woody Guthrie.......
DOG:Excellent uptempo song "Dog is happy, all eyes empty,dog is fully drained of all our pains,Dog is happy,happy,happy,where are you Dog? Come talk to me." THINK OF THE KIDS IN AFRIC Political song from old hardcore set. "You kids to day have it so easy,computer games,Guess jeans,and MTV,Africans still skin animal hides and they don't have an increase in teenage suicide."WISHES FOR THE SIXTIES: Peter Gunnish hard rocker."Paisleys and pastels adorn her body,plastic beads and big earrings look groovy,but her views are skewered by the scythe of false perceptions gleaned from from her insulated life.".....................
These guys rip live!!! You can probably find this tape in Sound Exchange or Waterloo Records............
–CAA

OASIS

Although I haven't seen many bands lately, here are some that I've enjoyed: Slackface, Ballad Shambles, Peace Corpse, and Shake Appeal.

And, Gawd, there's more n on the way, starting tonight, wit Glitch Records 45th annive party at the Back Room, with W the Dog, Peace Corp and the T Also, Big Twist and the M Fellows will be at Antone's.

the Musical Melting Pot
Various artists
Glitch Records
LP and cassette only
★ ★ ½

Local entrepreneur Keith Ayres' Glitch Records label has been putting together compilation records of obscure Austin bands since 1985, usually with mixed results. *Texas — The Musical Melting Pot*, the fourth in the series, again is a hit-and-miss affair, but the ratio of hits is down a bit from the impressive second and third samplers.

Ayres should be commended for bringing greater exposure to bands that otherwise have received little public notice. But sometimes the reason the bands on the Glitch samples are relatively unknown is because their music simply doesn't warrant much attention, and that's the case a little too often on this record.

Ayres seems to have an affinty for songs geared toward generic album rock stations, because about half the tunes on *The Musical Melting Pot* are of that dubious persuasion (which raises some questions about the accuracy of the record's title). Johnny Law's *Remember the Night* and the Titans' *Do It Right*, featured back-to-back on side one, are the most obvious examples, with the latter sounding like a cut from the soundtrack of a bad teen-age romance/tragedy flick.

Ring Theatre's *Shot* and the Rivals' *The Bullet and the Lie*, placed consecutively on side two, are similarly straightforward but mediocre rockers. Ring Theatre's politically oriented lyrics at least make an effort to present something more worthwhile, but the band bites off more than it can chew in its attempt to call for world peace and indict insincere leaders. Only through the more

personal perspective used in the song's tuneful break does the group manage to bring some sort of focus to its ideas.

Two of the best cuts come from the two non-Austin bands featured on the sampler, Dallas' October 8 and San Marcos' Second Glance. October 8's *Capitalism* is by far the catchiest tune on the album, though its lyrics don't run as deeply as the title might suggest. Second Glance's *Country Punkin'* is a rambunctiously fun, if ultimately disposable, cowpunk rave-up.

The Weeds' *Ice Age* and Peace Corps' *In a Cocked Rifle's Crack* are the best representations of Austin's garage/underground scene. Both are solid examples of simple but distinctive rock 'n' roll, with the latter's chorus particularly powerful and memorable.

The synth-pop diversions of European Sex Machine's *I Hear That* provide the only real evidence of a "musical melting pot" on the album, but it's not an especially noteworthy number. Last and least, though it's placed first on the record, is the juvenile *Kick 'em in the Ass* by Los Deflectors, which could have been an amusing wisecrack's update of Johnny Paycheck's *Take this Job and Shove It* if it weren't just plain stupid.

— Peter Blackstock

Worth a note

been that its music lacked emotion ... ing. Fortunately, singer/guitarist Berbrecht often spiced his lyrics with iro... self-deprecating humor, *enough irony* ... n up the combination of cold, percolat... nthesizers and drum machines. Al...'s wicked guitar strokes even did the... to warm the tone.

...wever, *Technique* departs from that ... What we get is sadly naive songs about ... and broken relationships. The lyrical iro... gone, leaving sappy and inane words to ... mpany a lifeless, chilly atmosphere. Key... d melodies wander aimlessly throughout ... y songs and even Peter Hook's wonderful ... playing can't save most of the songs. ...'s easier to pick the nice moments in ... hnique, because there are so many bad

ones. *Time*, the first song, starts with Albrecht yelling "You're much too young/to be a part me." Mounds of synthesizers that ..., soak and buzz, march along with a ..., infectious dance rhythm. And the following ... *All The Way*, provides strong melody ... and most of the release's insightful lyrics ... Albrecht says that "it takes years to find th...ve/ to be apart from what you know" ... The Way. However, the melody will stro... Like Heal...emind some of the Cure's *Just Like Heal* ...ngle. They are almost identical. Other th...ese two strengths, *Technique* has to be co...red a disappointment. If anything, this i... backward for what used to be one of roc... forward-looking groups. Complacency... ad thing.

— Michael T. Lyttle

SKIN & BONES

Tape and Record Reviews

LIVING IN A BOURGEOIS TOWN—PEACE CORPS

Ginsburg, Huang, Cooley, & Jones

LIVING IN A BOURGEOIS TOWN—PEACE CORPS

PEACE CORPS

LIVING IN A BOURGEOIS TOWN—

YUPPIE POSTER CHILD

The first time I saw Peace Corps I had walked in on a set they were playing at the Steamboat. I caught about half the set, and afterwards spoke to the lead singer. When I asked if they had a tape out, he laughed openly and then managed to tell me where I could buy a copy. The next day I bought it - Poster Yuppie Child. (I see now why he laughed.) I think they recorded it at home, and you can tell. The quality is not that great. The music on the other hand is good. I'm not into the Vegas nightclub sound too much, as several of their songs seem to be, but with Peace Corps, they've added something to it. Some of their songs are bawdy comedy, like "Watch her Squat", "Dog", and closer to home, "Wishes for the Sixties"; but most of their songs chronicle a time we live in, with "Think of the kids in Africa", "Pastures of Plenty", and "The Pinacle to the Panhandle" which tells about trailer homes in barren fields and the hungry and the homeless. Except for beating you over the head with the point in some songs, like "Dress Code", historians perhaps will look to P.C. for a piece of our history (granted our sons and daughters are allowed one.)

A short few weeks ago they released a studio tape, Living in a Bourgeois Town, in which they continued their "sufferage crusade". The quality is much better than the earlier tape. The vocals however are semi-overpowering and might put some people off. I don't mind personally though, accepting that I would appreciate a more hard-core sound. The only song appearing on both tapes is "Pastures of Plenty".

Several songs hit with local times, like "Alien" and "Fidelity Employee" telling about "cushy fools" walking through life without a clue. "Menage a Trios" on the other hand gives you back that bawdy comedy in contrast with their other songs. Both good tapes, both available around town. I suggest you try them out.

YUPPIE POSTER CHILD

PEACE CORPS

LiVE ReViews

The Hostages & Peace Corps at the Loft 2/26/88

The Loft is a dark club on Sixth Street with colored lights, a disco ball, and Black Label beer for a dollar. At midnight the Hostages came on. They are a three man band whose singer-guitar player looks like the guy from T-Rex. The music is kind of heavy-metal blues, with simple lyrics and lots of lead guitar. One cool song was Graveyard Man, where the guy made his guitar sound like an ambulance siren. They need to be tighter, but I liked the band and their songs and the girls in black miniskirts dancing to them. Peace Corps started playing about 2:30am. They are one of my favorite local bands. Back when they were Peace Corpse they were kind of hardcore, but now they have diversified into folk, jazz, and sometimes the Holiday Inn lounge sound. I like them best when they rock out. The songs have socially relevant themes like poverty, hunger, illegal aliens, and urine. They sounded pretty good, although the sax was kind of overpowering, and were fun onstage. Peace Corps is worth checking out.

-Greg Jones-

Austin's Only All-Music Magazine

Glitch news

VOL. IV NO.5
June 1988

LOCAL NOTES

By Keith A. Ayres

Glitch Sampler No.4 is beginning to take shape, but it is not too late to submit a 2-3 song demo tape of your band. Thus far I have received demos from Ring Theatre, EKU 28, the Weeds, the Titans, the Breed, the Colours, Peace Corps, the Quitters, Guardez Lou, the Mind Splinters, the Solid Senders, the Cats, the Things, Montage, the Crank and many others. You have until Dec. 31, 1987 to get your tape in. Bands that the Glitchmeister wants to include on the latest installment are; Peace Corps, the Weeds, Ring Theartre, the Rivals, Johnny Law, The Titans and October 8. The other three slots are still up for grabs. Any last minute suggestions or submissions can be mailed to: Glitch Sampler #4• PO Box 4429• Austin, TX 78765

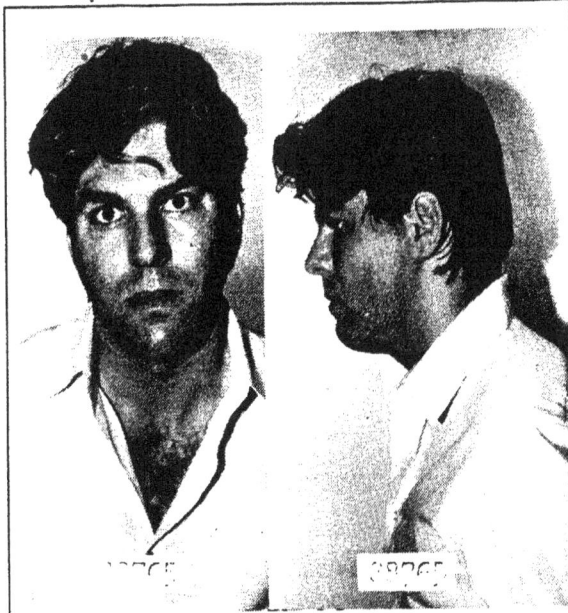

Ken Jones, singer/songwriter of Peace Corps. phots by D. Wilson

Ken Jones of Peace Corps has a record now, only it's not the kind that you can put on the turntable. It seems as though Jones and his buddy Byron Siren Scott were on there way to Corky's brew ha-ha at the Ritz on Tuesday March 29 when Jones, who was driving his 1988 Olds '88, took a corner too wide and was spotted by the law. Ken was promptly pulled over and as the result of a routine check, two unpaid speeding violations and a hot check popped up on the computer. The next thing Jones knew he was handcuffed and checked in to the posh Travis couty Jail to spend the night in the luxurious Drunk Tank. While on his overnight dream vacation, Jones made the acquaintance of another jailbird that had been arrested during the riot that took place in Corpus Christi over springbreak. As the result of another routine check the police found out Jone's acquaintance had allegedly violated his child support payments. Amazing what one can find out in a routine check. Oh yeah, Jones was released the next morning and he paid the outstanding fines.

SEPTEMBER 1988

PEACE CORPS

Peace Corps (pronounced Corpse) was formed during the Rock n' heyday of the Beach Cabaret, a now defunct Austin nightclub credited as being one of the first gigs for many Austin Rock bands including the Reivers and the Texas Instruments. Peace Corps was formed by some bored bartenders at the Beach and who started gigging to relieve the tension created by working as a bartender at the Beach Since those early days vocalist Ken Jones along with guitarist Mitch Ginsburg, bassist Gene Huang, and drummist Rob Cooley (who has been moonlighting with Not For Sale of Rabid Cat fame) have continued to churn out tw demented tapes containing some totally twisted words and music. The tapes titles are Yuppie Poster Child and Living

Peace Corps.   photo by David W

In A Bourgeois Town. Vocalist/lyricist Ken Jones has also released a solo project tape called, A Distant Land To Ros Peace Corps has achieved acceptance into the Austin club scene by landing gigs at Steamboat 1874, Liberty Lunch, Continental Club, the Backroom, the Black Cat Lounge, Fajita Flats, the Loft, the Beach, the Cave Club, and Big Mamou. Watch for Peace Corps appearing at a venue in j neighborhood soon.

RECOMMENDED

Austin American-Statesman

Best bets

On the town

Glitch Records is having a five-year anniversary party at the Back Room with Water the Dog, Peace Corps and Titans, starting at 10 p.m. Peace Corps, which just added guitarist Byron Scott from Do Dat, is changing its name to Peace Corp., meaning Peace Corporation. The Cover Girls touring dance band is at Stardust, Chicago's Big Twist and the Mellow Fellows are at Antone's, Grains of Faith and Damaged Goods are at the Texas Tavern, Mannish Boys are at the Continental Club, Agony Column is at Liberty Lunch, and Moments Notice is at the Black Cat Lounge. Ed Miller is at the Cactus Cafe, Blue Plate Special is at the Shark's Club, Tropical Vibes is at Mercado Caribe, and the Austin Lounge Lizards are at Threadgill's supper show.

★ THE AUSTIN ★ CHRONICLE

GLITCH ANNIVERSARY PARTY: WATER THE DOG, PEACE CORPS, & THE TITANS

Back Room, Wednesday 26

Has it really been five years since we first started seeing copies of the enigmatic *Ten Austin Groups in Black & White* floating around? Head Glitch man Keith Ayres says it has, and he should know, for in the time between then and now, he has gone on to release (by the time you read this) three more compilations and get his syndicated radio special "Austin Alternatives" off the ground and onto radio playlists around the country. This Back Room bash will not only celebrate five years of Glitch mania but will also herald the arrival of his latest compilation, *Texas — The Musical Melting Pot*, due out shortly. That effort will include tracks by these three bands, as well as new songs from the Weeds, Ring Theatre, the Rivals, Los Deflectors, and others.

Austin's Only All-Music Magazine
Glitch news

Live Reviews

**WATER THE DOG, PEACE CORP, the TITANS
GLITCH RECORDS 5th ANNIVERSARY PARTY
the BACKROOM, AUSTIN, TX. 10/26/88**

This evening marked a milestone for the Glitch Records folks, namely Keith A. Ayres. Congrats are in order for being able to keep his Glitch Record Company growing for five years. To celebrate the event Ayres threw a party at the Backroom and had three hot rock bands perform. Over 200 people attended and had a fantastic time.

The Titans opened with a tight set of 60's sounding originals including a rousing version of "Do It Right" which appears on the fourth Glitch Sampler.

Next up was the newly re-organized Peace Corp fronted by the stalwart Ken Jones (lead vocals) joined by PC veteran bassist Mitch Ginsburg. The new members in the band included Byron Scott (formerly with Do Dat and Pez) on guitar and Greg "Psycho-Hippie" Jones (formerly with the Bloodsucking Go-Devils) spanking the skins. Peace Corp turned in a credible set that featured songs like "Occupied America" from their cassette entitled "Living in A Bourgeois Town".

Water the Dog finished off the show with a powerful set of great original tunes. With songs like "Ecstacy," "My House" and "Box" the band got the audience up on the dance floor shaking. Craig Smith handled the vocal chores while being supported by; the "Tonemaster" Mike Tamas on guitar, Brian Crockett on bass and keys, and Bryan Kealing tying the group together with his phenominal drumming.

Great bands, great music, and a great audience. All in all, the 5th Anniversary Glitch Party was a success.

--Ward Rhodes

KAZI RADIO BENEFIT
Ritz Theater, Friday 13

With seemingly more lives than a dozen black cats, the Ritz Theater is once again among the living, thanks to Michael Barker, and one of its first gestures upon its resurrection will be to pay tribute and benefit to KAZI Radio, one of Austin's bastions of independent music exposure. In aid of this community radio station, a rather diverse quartet of local talent has been assembled — including lively funksters Bad Mutha Goose, soothing chainsaw bumpkins the Hickoids, plus the hard edged garage buzz of the Weeds and Peace Corpse. Also on hand will be commemorative T-shirts designed by Micael Priest, and, what KAZI cozily terms "cheap, cheap beer."

YO! BENEFIT TIME: Former Loft proprietor **Michael Barker** reopens the Ritz next Friday (the 13th), with a KAZI benefit coordinated by station deejays **Ron Lipeic** and **Roland Shield**. For a $5 cover, attendees at the reopening will get to see **Bad Mutha Goose, the Weeds, Hickoids and Peace Corps.**

On the town

The newly reopened Ritz Theatre on Sixth Street features a benefit for radio station KAZI-FM (88.7) with the Hickoids, Bad Mutha Goose, the Weeds, and Peace Corps. Zulu Time plays its final show with Van Wilks at Steamboat. Butch Hancock begins a two-night stand at the Cactus Cafe. The Chris Thomas Blues Band plays from 9:30 p.m. to 11 p.m. at the Black Cat Lounge, with Erik Moll and the Erik Hokkanen band taking over for the late-night set. Club Cairo's

Music News

By Luke Torn

November 13, 1987

On the town

. . . Ken Jones from the band Peace Corps also has a new cassette LP available shortly. Entitled *A Distant Land To Roam*, the songs mark Jones' foray into a tune called the includes acoustic music — he includes a tune called "Song To Jimmie," in honor of country music — and includes Go- legend Jimmie Rodgers — and includes Go- Walter Daniels of the Bloodsucking Devils on harmonica and flute on some tracks . . .

. . . whose *Yuppie Poster Child* cassette is available at area record stores, is at Big Mamou. The Peace Corps. available at area

Austin Chronicle / Austin American Statesman

Austin American-Statesman

Best bets — John Bryant

On the town

The Circle Jerks, a California rock band that has put out six albums, will be at Liberty Lunch to play cuts from their newest record, *VI*. The Weeds are on a double bill at Steamboat with Peace Corps, which get good reviews with their live shows. "These guys rip!" one critic says. Rufus KYT is at

On the town

The Wild Seeds are at Big Mamou, David "Fathead" Newman is at Antone's, Doug Sahm is at the Hole in the Wall, and Do Dat is at the Ritz Theater with the Peace Corps. Katy

On the town

The Peace Corps, whose *Yuppie Poster Child* cassette is available at area record stores, is at Big Mamou with the metal funk band Do Dat. The Hickoids are at Liberty Lunch with Loco Gringos and the Weeds for an

On the town

The Neville Brothers return to Liberty Lunch, with Moving Parts opening the 10 p.m. show. Lou Ann Barton and Bill Carter and the Blame are back at Antone's, Texas Instruments, Hundredth Monkey and the Wigglies are at Big Mamou, Do Dat and Peace Corps are at the Ritz, jazz trumpeter

On the town

Singer-songwriter R.C. Banks of Zydeco Ranch, also known as Randy, is doing a rare gig under his own name to celebrate his new album on the Amazing Records label. The concert is at Big Mamou, with folks like Ronnie Lane doing back-up vocals. The Def MFs are at the Ritz with the Peace Corps. Lance Keltner is at the Back Room. Rev. Horton Heat is at the

On the town

Junior "Shotgun" Walker and the All Stars are at Antone's, the Untouchables — a flashy, 9-piece West Coast ska band — is at the Cave Club, and the Wagoneers are at the Hole in the Wall. Hundredth Monkey and Wednesday Week are at the Texas Tavern, the Ideals, Bloodsucking Go-Devils and Peace Corps are at the Ritz, the Tremors are at the Coyote Club, Butch Hancock is at Big

Onward to The Weekend

NIGHTLIFE

the Peace Corps will have a tape release party and concert at 5 p.m. at Inner Sanctum.

Peace Corps, with Ken Jones and Gene Huang, perform Friday at the Loft.

Music News
By Luke Torn

. . . **Ken Jones** from the band **Peace Corps** also has a new cassette LP available shortly. Entitled *A Distant Land To Roam*, the songs mark Jones' foray into acoustic music — he includes a tune called "Song To Jimmie," in honor of country legend **Jimmie Rodgers** — and includes **Walter Daniels** of the **Bloodsucking Go-Devils** on harmonica and flute on some tracks . . .

!ive shots

December 18, 1987

Gettin' some toothy action from his strings — Mitch Ginsberg of Peace Corps at the Ritz.

PHOTOS BY DAVID L. WILSON

Peace Corps have finished their newest cassette, *Bourgeois Town*, recorded at Lone Star Studios

The **Peace Corps** celebrates the release of their newest tape with a release party on Feb. 26 at Inner Sanctum Records and a show that night at the Loft. . .

Also around the studios, **Tanz Waffen** and **Mark of Kane** are working on projects at Cedar Creek, while **Peace Corps** have finished their newest cassette, *Bourgeois Town*, recorded at Lone Star Studios . . .

Peace Corpse have a new cassette, *Yuppie Poster Child*, out soon . . .

THE COMPILATION BLUES: The final cuts have been made and head Glitchman **Keith Ayres** is about to begin production work on his newest sampler — *Texas, The Musical Melting Pot* — the fourth such collection in the series. The 10 mostly undocumented bands set to appear on the record include the **Weeds**, **Ring Theatre**, the **Rivals** (currently MIA and seeking a new bass player), **Johnny Law**, the **Titans**, **Peace Corps**, **Los Deflectors**, and three out-of-town acts, **Second Glance** (San Marcos), **October 8** (Dallas), and **Mulberry Jane** (Houston).

In the Studio

Compiled by Roland Swenson

LONE STAR RECORDING: Guardez Lou (indie LP), Peace Corps (demo), Progress (demo); W_____ _____ Posse (12-inch).

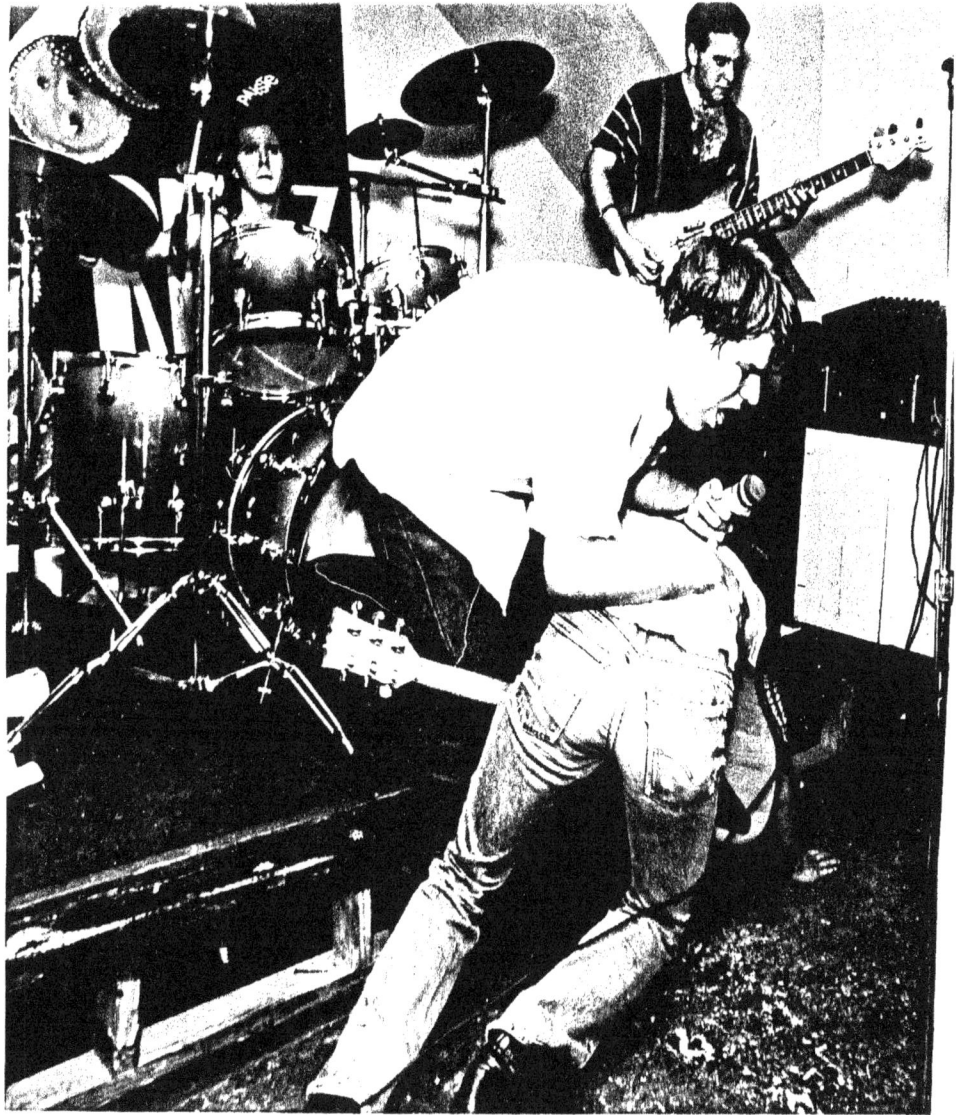

PEACE CORPS would like to thank the Austin Chronicle, the Austin American-Statesman, the Daily Texan, Fatalist Monthly and Carlton of ST 37, David Wilson for the front and back photos; the clubs we've played: The Ritz, Steamboat, Big Mamou, The Cave Club, Fajita Flats, the Loft, Liberty Lunch, The Black Cat, the Beach RIP and the Continental Club RIP; and all the people who've checked us out and enjoyed what they saw.

Woodshock

Woodshock '86 was presented by El Jefe Records, (comprised of Mike Alvarez and Jeff Smith (Matako Mazuri Records, Hickoids) who were still riding high on the Woodshock '85 release, and it saw a change in venues from the Hurlbut Ranch near Dripping Springs to camp Ben McCulloch which is located 10.5 miles off Highway 290 West on FM 1826. Woodshock '86 offered camping, swimming (at your own risk), food (BYOB), and of course the usual deluge of rock music, *LIVE* rock music. Advance tickets were up to $5.00 in '86 and $6.00 at the door. Bands included: Ice 9, Peace Corpse, Oboyo, the Dig, Barking Spiders, Guardez Lou, Get Smart, Black Spring, Celebrities, Do Dat, Nice Strong Arm, Poison 13, Last Will, Ideals, Strappados, Not For sale, Offenders, Raging Woodies, Minus Grace, Butthole Surfers, the Texas Instruments, Scratch Acid, Dino Lee, Screws, U-men, and the Hickoids.

So the 1987 Woodshock will once again be held at the Hurlbut Ranch, with 'Shock mainstays like the Hickoids, the Texas Instruments and Zeitgeist performing. Some other local bands involved include the Weeds, X-Communicated, Peace Corpse, Agony Column, the Bloodsucking Go-Devils, Do Dat, Guardez Lou, the Ideals, Dig, Not For Sale and others.

Photo by Rain Dog/Flying Horse magazine

Flying Horse
49 songs, 1.4 days, 1.89 GB

Name	Time	Album	Artist
Live at 617 W 24th 1/2 B	24:49	Flying Horse – Blood Sucking Go D...	Blood Sucking Go Devils
Side 1	23:21	Flying Horse – Do Dat – Studio	Do Dat
Side 1 – Strappados Interview	45:19	Flying Horse – Interview & Live at t...	Strappados, Peace Corp
Side 2	47:09	Flying Horse – Interview & Live at t...	Strappados, Peace Corp
Side 1	46:51	Flying Horse – Last day at the Beac...	Ideals
Side 2	45:42	Flying Horse – Last day at the Beac...	Ideals
Side 1	46:48	Flying Horse – Live at the Beach 1	Last Will, NSA, Vertibeads, Texas In...
Side 2	43:43	Flying Horse – Live at the Beach 1	Last Will, NSA, Vertibeads, Texas In...
Side 1 – Black String	45:40	Flying Horse – Live at the Beach 2	Black String, Peace Corpse
Side 2 – Peace Corpse	45:31	Flying Horse – Live at the Beach 2	Black String, Peace Corpse
Side 1	45:59	Flying Horse 1	Ken Jones, Bisqcuit, Poison 13, Pez
Side 2	7:07	Flying Horse 1	Ken Jones, Bisqcuit, Poison 13, Pez
Side 1	46:43	Flying Horse 2 Live at Tacoland	First band ?, Strappados
Side 2 – First band ?, Strappados Li...	47:02	Flying Horse 2 Live at Tacoland	First band ?, Strappados
Side 1	46:33	Flying Horse 3	Peace Corps, Jeff Daniels, Year Zero
Side 2	46:38	Flying Horse 3	Peace Corps, Jeff Daniels, Year Zero
Side 1	46:40	Flying Horse 3a	Peace Corps, Jeff Daniels, Year Zero
Side 2	46:58	Flying Horse 3a	Peace Corps, Jeff Daniels, Year Zero
Side 1	47:09	Flying Horse 3b	Do Dat
Side 1	46:52	Flying Horse 3c	Do Dat, Ken Jones, Bad Mutha Goose
Side 2	47:00	Flying Horse 3c	Do Dat, Ken Jones, Bad Mutha Goose
Side 1	44:18	Flying Horse 3d	Peter Beck, Hickoids, G.F. Wright
Side 2	1:00:35	Flying Horse 3d	Peter Beck, Hickoids, G.F. Wright
4 Track Master	30:49	Flying Horse 7/18/86 Tape 5	Ken Jones, U–Men
4 Track Master	11:36	Flying Horse 7/18/86 Tape 6	U–Men
Side 1	51:03	Flying Horse 7/18/86 2 Track master	Ken Jones, U–Men
Side 2	11:22	Flying Horse 7/18/86 2 Track master	Ken Jones, U–Men
4 Track Master	46:41	Flying Horse 7/18/86 Tape 1	Joey G., Blood Sucking Go Devils
Side 1	43:47	Flying Horse 7/18/86 Tape 1 2 Tra...	Joey G., Blood Sucking Go Devils
Side 2	44:08	Flying Horse 7/18/86 Tape 1 2 Tra...	Joey G., Blood Sucking Go Devils
4 Track Master	46:32	Flying Horse 7/18/86 Tape 2	Blood Sucking Go Devils, June
Side 1	49:25	Flying Horse 7/18/86 Tape 2 2 Tra...	NSA, Fred Reading, Ward, The Dig
Side 2	43:22	Flying Horse 7/18/86 Tape 2 2 Tra...	NSA, Fred Reading, Ward, The Dig
4 Track Master	1:09:37	Flying Horse 7/18/86 Tape 4	The Dig
Side 1	37:26	Flying Horse June '86	Scratch Acid, Ken Jones
Side 2	45:51	Flying Horse June '86	Scratch Acid, Ken Jones
Side 1 – Ideals	44:54	Flying Horse June 86	Ideals, Liz B, Gerald
Side 2 – Liz B, Gerald	43:02	Flying Horse June 86	Ideals, Liz B, Gerald
Side 1	46:57	Flying Horse Live at the Beach 3	Go Devils
Side 2	46:41	Flying Horse Live at the Beach 3	Go Devils
Side 1	51:39	Flying Horse Live For the Austin Be...	Various
Side 1	46:35	Flying Horse Record	Various
4 Track Master	51:00	Flying Horse Tape 3	Nice Stong Arm, Ward 69–86
Side 1 Strappados	41:34	Flying Horse Woodshock Benefit 1	Strappados, Hickoids
Side 2 Hickoids	41:40	Flying Horse Woodshock Benefit 1	Strappados, Hickoids
Side 1	51:01	Flying Horse Woodshock Benefit 2	Unknown, Undocumented
Side 2	30:00	Flying Horse Woodshock Benefit 2	Unknown, Undocumented
Side 1 – NSA	47:17	Flying Horse Woodshock Benefit 3	Nice Strong Arm, Michael Lawson
Side 2 – Michael Lawson	44:52	Flying Horse Woodshock Benefit 3	Nice Strong Arm, Michael Lawson

Flying Horse
49 songs, 1:11:12:52 total time, 1.89 GB

Name	Time	Album	Artist
Flying Horse - Blood Sucking Go D...	24:49	Flying Horse - Blood Sucking Go D...	Blood Sucking Go Devils
Flying Horse - Do Dat - Studio	23:21	Flying Horse - Do Dat - Studio	Do Dat
Flying Horse - Interview & Live at t...	45:19	Flying Horse - Interview & Live at t...	Strappados, Peace Corp
Flying Horse - Interview & Live at t...	47:09	Flying Horse - Interview & Live at t...	Strappados, Peace Corp
Flying Horse - Last day at the Beac...	46:51	Flying Horse - Last day at the Beac...	Ideals
Flying Horse - Last day at the Beac...	45:42	Flying Horse - Last day at the Beac...	Ideals
Flying Horse - Live at the Beach 1a	46:48	Flying Horse - Live at the Beach 1a	Last Will, NSA, Vertibeads, Texas In...
Flying Horse - Live at the Beach 1b	43:43	Flying Horse - Live at the Beach 1b	Last Will, NSA, Vertibeads, Texas In...
Flying Horse - Live at the Beach 2a ...	45:40	Flying Horse - Live at the Beach 2a	Black String, Peace Corpse
Flying Horse - Live at the Beach 2b ...	45:31	Flying Horse - Live at the Beach 2b	Black String, Peace Corpse
Flying Horse 1a	45:59	Flying Horse 1a	Ken Jones, Bisqcuit, Poison 13, Pez
Flying Horse 1b	7:07	Flying Horse 1b	Ken Jones, Bisqcuit, Poison 13, Pez
Flying Horse 2 Live at Tacoland a Fi...	46:43	Flying Horse 2 Live at Tacoland a	First band ?, Strappados
Flying Horse 2 Live at Tacoland b St...	47:02	Flying Horse 2 Live at Tacoland b	First band ?, Strappados
Flying Horse 3 a	46:33	Flying Horse 3 a	Peace Corps, Jeff Daniels, Year Zero
Flying Horse 3 b	46:38	Flying Horse 3 b	Peace Corps, Jeff Daniels, Year Zero
Flying Horse 3a a	46:40	Flying Horse 3a a	Peace Corps, Jeff Daniels, Year Zero
Flying Horse 3a b	46:58	Flying Horse 3a b	Peace Corps, Jeff Daniels, Year Zero
Flying Horse 3b a	47:09	Flying Horse 3b a	Do Dat
Flying Horse 3c a	46:52	Flying Horse 3c a	Do Dat, Ken Jones, Bad Mutha Goose
Flying Horse 3c b	47:00	Flying Horse 3c b	Do Dat, Ken Jones, Bad Mutha Goose
Flying Horse 3d a	44:18	Flying Horse 3d a	Peter Beck, Hickoids, G.F. Wright
Flying Horse 3d b	1:00:35	Flying Horse 3d b	Peter Beck, Hickoids, G.F. Wright
Flying Horse 7/18/86 Tape 5 4 Tr...	30:49	Flying Horse 7/18/86 Tape 5	Ken Jones, U-Men
Flying Horse 7/18/86 Tape 6 4 Tr...	11:36	Flying Horse 7/18/86 Tape 6	U-Men
Flying Horse 7/18/86 2 Track mast...	51:03	Flying Horse 7/18/86 2 Track mast...	Ken Jones, U-Men
Flying Horse 7/18/86 2 Track mast...	11:22	Flying Horse 7/18/86 2 Track mast...	Ken Jones, U-Men
Flying Horse 7/18/86 Tape 1 4 Tra...	46:41	Flying Horse 7/18/86 Tape 1	Joey G., Blood Sucking Go Devils
Flying Horse 7/18/86 Tape 1 2 Tra...	43:47	Flying Horse 7/18/86 Tape 1 2 Tra...	Joey G., Blood Sucking Go Devils
Flying Horse 7/18/86 Tape 1 2 Tra...	44:08	Flying Horse 7/18/86 Tape 1 2 Tra...	Joey G., Blood Sucking Go Devils
Flying Horse 7/18/86 Tape 2 4 Tra...	46:32	Flying Horse 7/18/86 Tape 2	NSA, Fred Reading, Ward, The Dig
Flying Horse 7/18/86 Tape 2 2 Tra...	49:25	Flying Horse 7/18/86 Tape 2 2 Tra...	NSA, Fred Reading, Ward, The Dig
Flying Horse 7/18/86 Tape 2 2 Tra...	43:22	Flying Horse 7/18/86 Tape 2 2 Tra...	NSA, Fred Reading, Ward, The Dig
Flying Horse 7/18/86 Tape 4 4 Tra...	1:09:37	Flying Horse 7/18/86 Tape 4	The Dig
Flying Horse June '86 a	37:26	Flying Horse June '86 a	Scratch Acid, Ken Jones
Flying Horse June '86 b	45:51	Flying Horse June '86 b	Scratch Acid, Ken Jones
Flying Horse June '86 c Ideals	44:54	Flying Horse June 86 c	Ideals, Liz B, Gerald
F ying Horse June '86 d Liz B, Gerald	43:02	Flying Horse June 86 d	Ideals, Liz B, Gerald
Flying Horse Live at the Beach 3 a	46:57	Flying Horse Live at the Beach 3 a	Go Devils
Flying Horse Live at the Beach 3 b	46:41	Flying Horse Live at the Beach 3 b	Go Devils
Flying Horse Live For the Austin Be...	51:39	Flying Horse Live For the Austin Be...	Various
Flying Horse Record	46:35	Flying Horse Record	Various
Flying Horse Tape 3 4 Track Master	51:00	Flying Horse Tape 3	Nice Stong Arm, Ward 69-86
Flying Horse Woodshock Benefit 1a...	41:34	Flying Horse Woodshock Benefit 1a	Strappados, Hickoids
Flying Horse Woodshock Benefit 1b...	41:40	Flying Horse Woodshock Benefit 1b	Strappados, Hickoids
Flying Horse Woodshock Benefit 2a...	51:01	Flying Horse Woodshock Benefit 2a	Unknown, Undocumented
Flying Horse Woodshock Benefit 2b...	30:00	Flying Horse Woodshock Benefit 2b	Unknown, Undocumented
Flying Horse Woodshock Benefit 3a...	47:17	Flying Horse Woodshock Benefit 3a	Nice Strong Arm, Michael Lawson
Flying Horse Woodshock Benefit 3b...	44:52	Flying Horse Woodshock Benefit 3b	Nice Strong Arm, Michael Lawson